· THE LAWS OF THE SUN ·

THE LAWS of the SUN

ONE SOURCE
ONE PLANET
ONE PEOPLE

Ryuho Okawa

IRH PRESS

IRH PRESS
New York . Tokyo

Distributed by Midpoint Trade Books. www.midpointtrade.com

Library of Congress Cataloging-in-Publication Data
ISBN 13: 978-1-937673-04-8
ISBN 10: 1-937673-04-9

Printed in China

Jacket Art and Design: LeVan Fisher Design
Book Design: Jennifer Daddio / Bookmark Design & Media Inc.
Jacket Imagery: Shutterstock / DrHitch and Shutterstock / Reistlin Magere

CONTENTS

CHAPTER ONE

THE SUN OF THE TRUTHS IS RISING

CHAPTER FOUR
THE ULTIMATE ENLIGHTENMENT

CHAPTER FIVE
THE GOLDEN AGES: THE HISTORY
OF HUMANKIND

CHAPTER SIX

THE PATH TO EL CANTARE

FOREWORD BY THE PUBLISHER

*"Don't be afraid of a terrible future. Destiny can
be created by your own ability, by your own efforts.
You can create yourself; you can create your
society, you can create the future of Earth."*
MASTER RYUHO OKAWA IN *FORECAST*

*I*t is always darkest just before dawn. The world is facing a turbulent age of economic, political, and religious challenges;
apocalyptic prophecies; and catastrophic natural disasters.
But we must remember that turbulent times precede great advances in human history. As we speak, the most glorious sun
ever beheld—the harbinger of a new golden era—is making
its way above the horizon. You will find some of this same
radiant light of God's Truths within the pages of *The Laws of
the Sun*.

Based on his miraculous ability to see the challenges
and accomplishments of past, present, and future millennia,
Master Ryuho Okawa has written this remarkable account of
the framework of God's Laws. Master Okawa explains how
and why God designed the universe and all things within it.
He shows us how living in accord with God's Truths gives

us the power to transform our planet, turning it away from catastrophe and straight toward love and acceptance between people of all religions and races. When Jews, Christians, Muslims, and Buddhists discover our common spiritual source, their hearts will be inspired to let go of millennia of conflict and finally forgive and embrace each other. As we make God's Truths part of our own wisdom, the world's economic and political leaders will find new solutions to international problems and help the global economy harness the engines of lasting prosperity, allowing people to pursue the American dream in *all* parts of the world. Through the power of the love and wisdom within us, we *will* defy doom-and-gloom prophecies. The key to bringing happiness to all of Earth is simple: we only need to realize how much God has been cherishing each one of us for infinite time, and emulate his merciful love in our own lives. As we come together as *one people,* from *one source,* on *one planet,* we will build a new era of spirituality based on God's Truths as they are revealed here in this transformative book.

Do not let the mystical aspect of this book put you off, or you will miss an extraordinary opportunity to bring insight, meaning, and peace into your life—to benefit from the answers to our most profound spiritual questions, recorded in this book through divine providence shortly after Master Ryuho Okawa attained enlightenment. When we leave this world, does consciousness simply come to an end, or do we begin an eternal life of the spirit? Is there truth in reincarnation? Or in the belief that we are all born of original sin? What if he could explain to us why there is a Heaven and a Hell, and what the afterlife is truly like? *The Laws of the Sun* not only provides answers to these age-old questions, but also reveals the hidden story of Earth's genesis; the Truths about Earth's intimate relationships with other parts of the universe; and the profound, untold history of humankind. Let the Truths in this book reveal to you both the challenges we will face together and the infinite glories of our wonderful future.

As these words resonate with your very soul, may you find new joy in your connection to the common source of all faiths and all living things.

AUTHOR'S NOTE

In August 1986, one month after I handed in my resignation to the trading company I had been working for, I started writing the book you now hold in your hands, *The Laws of the Sun*. Although I had previously published several compilations of spiritual messages through a small publishing company specializing in spirituality, I thought that I was not yet in a position to guide others, and in truth, I had only a vague idea of how wide the scope of our activities would become in the years ahead. I hadn't even decided what to name the spiritual organization I was going to establish. I was thinking about naming it "Happy Science," but when I told this to the publisher, I met with strong opposition. He said an organization with a name like that would never be successful, so we ended up parting ways. Fortunately, *The Laws of the Sun* spoke to a lot of readers, many of whom decided to join Happy Science. The fact that *The Laws of the Sun*, written twenty-five years ago, still remains the fundamental text of Happy Science shows that I had achieved a very high level of enlightenment at an early stage. Today, this single book underlies all of my teachings at Happy Science and serves as the basis for the more than nine hundred books I have published.*

The Laws of the Sun is the first book that I wrote entirely using automatic writing. I simply held a pen in my hand and let it write the manuscript of its own volition, filling five pages every hour. The manuscript was exactly three hundred pages long,[1] which means that I wrote the entire book in sixty hours. Not only was this an amazing mystical experience, but it was also incredibly convenient. I could write without having to use my brain, so apart from giving me stiff shoulders, this technique wasn't the least bit taxing. However, as Happy Science grew, I became increasingly busy, and soon I could not even spend the time needed for automatic writing. Now, I mainly publish books based on transcripts of my talks. Looking back, I see that *The Laws of the Sun* has irreplaceable value not just for its ideas, but also as my first handwritten book.

Another thing that makes *The Laws of the Sun* special is that it describes Creation much the way Genesis does in the Christian Bible, although in very different terms. *The Laws of the Sun* shows that the history of religion was actually shaped by Great Guiding Spirits and Angels of Light, who appeared throughout history to save the people of this world. In other

---

* As of June 2012.

words, all the world's religions, including Buddhism, Christianity, and Islam, as well as local and regional religions such as Shintoism in Japan, were created by Divine Spirits sent to Earth by God, whom we also call Buddha.

All religions have the same roots. They may take different forms depending on the characteristics and experiences of the people who founded them, or the circumstances and eras the founders were born in, but fundamentally, religions should not be in conflict with one another or bring confusion to this world. Instead of suggesting that one god is better than another, *The Laws of the Sun* shows us that all religions come from one source, which is one of the most significant teachings in this book.

I also describe how different Grand Spirits have descended to Earth to bring about the rise of past civilizations that are often regarded merely as myths. I reveal the fact that ten spirits exist in the ninth dimension, and that they were responsible for guiding the civilizations of Lamudia, Mu, and Atlantis. Although I relied on my intuition to write this, I was able to verify the authenticity of this revelation: spirits from the ninth dimension spoke through me in 2010, answering questions posed by various interviewers, while the entire process was videotaped. During the course of these interviews, each of the ninth-dimension spirits revealed who they are, how they think, and how they contributed to the flourishing of these civilizations.

At the time I wrote this book, I had never given a public lecture and didn't have any experience as a religious teacher. I gave my first talk on November 23, 1986, the same year I wrote this book. It was more like a discussion session than a lecture, but in Buddhist terms, the moment could be described as "the First Turning of the Dharma Wheel"— my initial step toward fulfilling my destiny. About ninety people gathered to listen to my first talk. I was very nervous, so I spoke quite fast, but this experience prepared me for my first public lecture on "The Principles of Happiness," which I gave on March 8, 1987, at the Ushigome Public Hall in Tokyo.

When we first began our activities, I wanted to limit the expansion of our movement, since I didn't have the practical knowledge necessary to manage a large religious group. I was very cautious at the beginning. My plan was to first establish the foundational teachings, then create a good management style, and only at that point expand the organization. With this strategy in mind, I wrote the trilogy of fundamental teachings—*The Laws of the Sun*, *The Golden Laws*, and *The Nine Dimensions* (originally titled *The Laws of Eternity*)—and then created the basic style for managing our movement. From then on, Happy Science grew rapidly. Within several years, I was giving talks at venues that could accommodate audiences of well over ten thousand people. Several years after that, I was lecturing to fifty thousand people at the Tokyo Dome. The rapid growth we achieved was extraordinary.

Before the rapid growth and success of Happy Science, however, I spent five and a half years accumulating spiritual wisdom and practical experiences. During this period, I recorded and studied the transcripts of spiritual messages from various Divine Spirits and developed the basic teachings of Happy Science. While I engaged in these intense spiritual experiences, I also continued to work hard at my job at the trading firm. This was a period of great spiritual discipline for me, the equivalent of the six years Shakyamuni Buddha spent after he left his life in the palace before attaining his great enlightenment.

I attained my great enlightenment on March 23, 1981. On the Monday afternoon, I received a clear message from Heaven that awakened me to my mission on Earth. I felt that some invisible being was there with me trying to tell me something. I grabbed some blank notecards, placed them in front of me, and held a pencil in my hand. Of its volition my hand began writing "Good news, Good news" on the cards. When it kept writing this message over and over again and didn't stop, I asked, "I've got the 'Good news' message; is there anything else you would like to tell me?" But my hand still kept writing "Good news, Good news." That was the only message I received on that day. It was the gospel of God telling me that something good was about to happen, that a new beginning was coming.

At first, I could receive messages from Heaven only through automatic writing, but as time went by, I became able to act as a conduit for the spoken word as well. I learned how to let spirits use my vocal cords, allowed these spirits to engage me in conversation, and conducted question-and-answer sessions in which I played the roles of both interviewer and interviewee. In this way, communication with the spirit world became part of my everyday life, as it has been for the past thirty years.

The next revelation I received from a spirit in Heaven was "love, nurture, and forgive others." I learned that these words were to be essential to my teachings, and they certainly took center stage in *The Laws of the Sun*. Many people suffer because they feel they are not being loved. The root cause of this distress comes from their desire to receive or obtain love from others. But from a religious perspective, true love is not the love you take; it's the love you give to others. Awakening to the nature of true love is the starting point of enlightenment. Giving love is the basis for every truly religious act. In Buddhism, the concept of love is often taken negatively, as it has a connotation of attachment to this world. But the love I am talking about is closer to the Buddhist idea of compassion. Compassion represents giving, much like the sun that shines and constantly provides us with its light. Giving love is an act that expresses God's mercy on a human level.

Of course it's important that we love our friends and those close to us, but we should also love those with whom we do not have any direct relationship, and do so without expecting anything in return. I call this first type of love *fundamental love*. Fundamental love is the first stage of love, which is followed by *spiritually nurturing love*. Spiritually nurturing love involves more than simply being kind to others. It requires us to teach and guide them so that they can grow spiritually. It gives us the power to improve the world, to make it a better place. This is the type of love you encounter on your path to becoming a leader of great character—a path that requires wisdom. Loving others with wisdom is a step higher than fundamental love.

So good leaders give a spiritually nurturing love, but when they acquire wisdom, they also develop a strong tendency to distinguish right from wrong, and consequently to judge people. This is true of all of us to a certain extent. For example, the more we study, or the more knowledge we acquire, the easier it becomes to identify lack of knowledge in others. So when you develop nurturing love, at some point you will find yourself passing judgments. When a company president sees his employees in the workplace, for example, he may sometimes feel that they are being unproductive; he might think, "They shouldn't be getting paid for goofing off." This is because the president has much more knowledge and experience than the employees. The employees may not be living up to his expectations; however, they are still in the development stage, so he should not judge them to be right or wrong. He must know that he is supposed to teach and guide them.

This leads us to a form of love that is even higher than the nurturing love of good leaders. This higher love is represented by the word *forgive* in "love, nurture, and forgive others." This is a very difficult level to attain, especially if you are in business. To reach this state of mind, you must awaken to the Truth that all human beings have a divine nature, the essence of God's nature, within them. When you realize this, you will know that all people have the potential to achieve enlightenment through their efforts. They have been born in this world to undergo spiritual training on Earth. They are your brothers and sisters, and like you, they are struggling to improve their souls by overcoming the difficulties and hardships that they face during the course of their lives.

You will also realize that at one time, you were all souls in Heaven, and that just as you have all been born into this world, some day you will all leave this world. When you awaken to the Truth that human beings undergo soul training through the cycle of reincarnation, you will attain the state of *forgiving love*, which surpasses the notion of right and wrong. This is a deeply religious state of mind.

One example of forgiving love can be found in the novel *Les Miserables*. The main character of the novel, Jean Valjean, steals some silverware from the house of a bishop, but the police catch him and bring him back to the bishop's house. When the police officer asks the bishop whether Jean Valjean stole his silverware, the bishop rescues him by telling the officer that the silverware was a gift, and that he even asked Jean Valjean to take silver candlesticks as well! Forgiven by the bishop, Jean Valjean reforms himself and eventually rises to become a mayor. People who have attained a truly religious state of mind, like the bishop in the novel, have the power to bring change to the hearts of others and to reform their lives. Even those who are criminals or villains from this world's standpoint of right and wrong can turn over a new leaf and become worthy of respect. This is the power of forgiving love.

In *The Laws of the Sun*, I discuss a stage of love higher than forgiving love: *love incarnate*. This higher love is an expression of compassion that can be seen in the lives of those great figures in history who shined light into people's hearts and became the source of people's joy. These people brought happiness to the world just by being born and living on Earth. One example is Jesus Christ, who only lived thirty-three years but became a light for the world for two thousand years. Another example is Mahatma Gandhi, honored in India as the Father of the Nation, who successfully fought against the British colonization of India through mass civil disobedience, a non-violent method that made a great impact on the whole world. Abraham Lincoln is another example. His terribly difficult mission was to lead during the American Civil War, end slavery, and unify the United States of America. These people shine out like brilliant stars in the history of humanity. The love they exemplify is love incarnate.

The developmental stages of love—fundamental love, spiritually nurturing love, forgiving love and love incarnate—integrate the teachings of love taught in Christianity and the teachings of enlightenment taught in Buddhism. There are different levels of enlightenment in Buddhism. The *Laws of the Sun* shows how each level of enlightenment corresponds to a stage of love, a correlation that became part of the basis of the fundamental teachings of Happy Science.

Some of the contents of *The Laws of the Sun* may be difficult for someone who is new to my teachings, but it's not necessary to understand all the details. I will be glad for you to see the basic relationship between enlightenment and love, and to understand that in spite of all the tragedies that occur in this world, God has never given up on us; this is why He has sent numerous Divine Spirits down to Earth to guide and save people throughout history.

The present age is no exception. With a population on

its way to ten billion, there is no way that God can sit still and not show us the path to salvation. Now is the moment for God's Truths to be taught and spread so as to bring hope and salvation to all who dwell on Earth. We are keenly aware that this is our mission and duty as a movement. I hope that you will read and enjoy *The Laws of the Sun* and find your way to making this world that we share as brothers and sisters into a better place.

PREFACE

—From the 1994 Japanese Edition—

It was back in September 1986 that I wrote *The Laws of the Sun*,* the first book that I published about my teachings. *The Laws of the Sun* sold millions of copies in paperback, and as a result, Happy Science and I became well-known throughout Japan. The English edition has also attracted avid readers throughout the world in major cities such as New York, London, Cairo, and Sydney; countries such as Sri Lanka; and the region of Tibet.

Since much has transpired over the past eight years, I have significantly revised this book that I cherish and am offering the revised edition through IRH Press. In 1986, Happy

---

* Ryuho Okawa, *Taiyō no Hō* [The Laws of the Sun] (Tokyo: Tsuchiya Shoten, 1987).

Science did not yet exist or have even a single follower. Now, Happy Science has grown into one of the largest religions in Japan. Meanwhile, my enlightenment has made further progress. I spent dozens of hours thoroughly investigating the spirit world to write this 1994 edition, and many new and valuable facts have come to light. In addition to these discoveries, I have added a detailed autobiography to chapter 6. I wrote this autobiography as objectively and straightfor-wardly as I could because I have found that some Japanese journalists and religious scholars have little appreciation for the virtue of humility.

The Laws of the Sun is a tremendously mystical book. To fully appreciate its wisdom, you must open your heart to the Truths that I reveal here and accept them in place of your *common-sense values*. I hope that, in the near future, my more than forty million readers will transform these Truths into the *standard values of the world*.

Ryuho Okawa
Founder and CEO
Happy Science Group
June 1994

THE SUN OF THE
TRUTHS IS RISING

1. The Sun of Buddha's Truths

The past, present, and future of humankind are tapestries that have been woven by the golden thread of the Truths of Buddha, whom we also call God. This heavenly thread is His mind, His creeds, and His very life, which is everywhere, flowing through the entire universe. Throughout history, this golden thread has provided us with cloaks to warm our hearts and spirits against the cold. One such garment of splendor was the teaching of Shakyamuni Buddha in India. Another was the teaching of Confucius in China. A third appeared in Palestine, when the Truths manifested as Jesus Christ's gospel of love.

Since the birth of time, great men and women have been

sent to bestow these garments upon the world in various shapes, sizes, and colors. In Japan, during the Heian period from 794 to 1185, the Buddhist monk Kūkai and others spread Buddhist teachings that nourished the human soul. During the Kamakura period, from 1185 to 1333, monks such as Hōnen, Shinran, Eisai, Dōgen, Myōe, Nichiren, and Ippen restored the teachings of Shakyamuni Buddha to prominence. And during the Muromachi period, from 1333 to 1573, Rennyo revived the teachings of Shin Buddhism. In other countries, other great leaders have provided similar blessings; certainly the teachings of such famous high monks as Nagarjuna of India and T'ien-t'ai Chih-i of China must be counted among these blessings. The works of these great men are all part of the heavenly fabric of Buddha's Truths.

Today, the emergence of Happy Science marks the fifth major religious movement in Japan[2] and with its arrival, the greatest masterpiece of the tapestries of Buddha's Truths is now on the brink of completion. This moment is an extraordinary display of Buddha's growing desire to protect our hearts from materialism and from the belief that our human existence ends with physical death. He is our great protector who is always providing our hearts with light and warmth, and today we see signs that the sun of His Truths is preparing to shine down upon us more brilliantly than ever before.

Certainly there have been periods when this sun was hidden, when rain lashed us from the skies and icy gusts of wind made us shiver in fear. At times, the sun of Buddha's Truths has seemed to keep its distance, and even to disappear altogether. Nevertheless, far above the thick sea of clouds that blocks our view, the golden orb has been faithfully emanating light. Even when chaos filled the Earth and turmoil filled people's minds—making it seem as though the light had vanished—thankfully, His rays never failed to pierce the clouds. For this is the light of salvation that rescues us from times of darkness and provides us the spiritual nourishment for life.

Today, the sun of Buddha's Truths has grown even larger and has begun to rise above the horizon with greater radiance than ever before. In this book, *The Laws of the Sun*, I describe this blazing beacon of new hope that has been bestowed upon our generation and all generations to come. This treasure has been hidden for more than two millennia—since the time of Shakyamuni Buddha. But now, as the sun of Buddha's Truths rises higher, its brilliant light emanates from a small corner of the world—Japan, the land of Shakyamuni Buddha's rebirth—and casts its radiance over the entire world. The sun of Buddha's Truths is rising, and before long, countless people will witness its glorious glow as it embraces the world with its magnificence.

The world today is waiting for this light, longing for Buddha's Truths to rise with the dawning sun and shatter the ramparts of darkness—the worldly delusions that humanity has formed throughout the ages. Triumphantly and with a mighty force, He will take His Will, His creeds, and His life to the limitless horizon of the universe.

I have written *The Laws of the Sun* in the earnest hope that you will join countless others in rising to this extraordinary occasion by making it your life's work to spread Buddha's Truths to all who long for spiritual nourishment. Every word in these pages is imbued with my wish to bring salvation to the world. It is my deepest hope that what you read here will become life-giving words of light for you, and for all our brothers and sisters on Earth.

2. What Is Buddha?

Have you ever wondered about the meaning of life? If so, what conclusions have you reached? In considering life in this three-dimensional world of ours, we must begin by defining it. Many people think of life as the brief handful of decades we spend between birth and death. If this is what you currently believe, then prepare yourself: this book will turn your entire worldview upside down.

If life were truly finite and ended in death, then once the body is cremated, only a few bones and a handful of ash would remain. And if this is really all that a life amounts to, why do we bother to put so much effort into it? Why do we sweat and toil in pursuit of our dreams? Why do we study so hard to educate ourselves? Why do we seek to deepen our wisdom and understanding about life? We do so because deep inside, we know the truth.

More than 2,500 years ago in India, Gautama Siddhartha—Shakyamuni Buddha—expounded and spread his teachings about Buddha's Truths. Throughout the eighty years of his lifetime, he tirelessly educated people about the purpose of life, the unique missions that all people are born with, and the existence of the other world, the spirit world.[3] Were all those teachings just an effort to fool people? Of course not. Nor were they ignorant statements rooted in a lack of sophistication or knowledge. Rather, they were the principles of a man who had attained enlightenment.

Skeptics may be proud of their intellectual sophistication, but can they credibly claim to have mastered greater Truths than Shakyamuni Buddha? If cynics insist that the teachings of Shakyamuni Buddha are false, then what about the Truths taught by Jesus Christ two thousand years ago and his belief in God? Are those teachings also meaningless? Covered in blood and sweat, Jesus prayed in the garden of Gethsemane and was crucified wearing a crown of thorns. Today, he is revered by more than a billion people. Jesus was a true envoy of the Truths, and those who write him off as a madman are the very people who ought to come forth and prove their sanity to the world.

Adherents of scientific rationalism say that they will believe in the existence of spirits only when they see them. However, as a simple matter of respect, they ought to look more closely at the wisdom of Christ and Shakyamuni Buddha, two great figures honored by humanity for millennia. The only way anyone could credibly dismiss the truth of their teachings is by proving that they have understood the wisdom of these figures thoroughly and discovered themselves to possess greater wisdom and saintliness. No one has ever done this, and no one ever will. In the mastery of Buddha's Truths, no one has ever surpassed Shakyamuni Buddha, who achieved the highest level of enlightenment, or Jesus Christ, who was guided by El Cantare, the core consciousness of Shakyamuni Buddha.

So don't fall prey to skepticism. Open the door to your mind, set yourself free from prejudice, and consider the teachings of Buddha in the true spirit of scientific inquiry. All of us encounter Him at some point on our journey through life. You only have to look around you to find clues that lead to His teachings, for they are scattered everywhere. He provides the greatest clues at birth and death, but we can also capture glimpses of Him in times of adversity and love.

Come, then, and join me in the pages ahead as we explore the question "What is Buddha?" and, in the process, find the meaning and purpose of our lives on Earth.

3. Being and Time

As you have surely observed, there is a universal law running through all of Creation. This is the law of constant change. From the moment of our birth, we, all creatures, and all objects under the generous and brilliant sun—human, animal, plant, microbe, and mineral—are governed by this law. What is the law of constant change? It describes the protean aspect of Creation: all things are in flux. Everything passes through the stages of birth, growth, decline, and death. The most obvious example is our own lives: we human beings are given life when we're born, develop into adults, gradually age, and eventually pass on from this world.

This law applies to all things, natural or manufactured. Take, for example, an automobile. A car comes into existence when it is assembled in a factory, provides transportation for a period of time until it begins to break down, and is eventually recycled. Plants go through the same process. A plant's life begins when it sprouts from a seed. Then, the sprout grows and blooms into beautiful flowers. The blossoms eventually wither, and the plant dies. Everything that exists in this world of the third dimension is in flux; everything passes through the four stages of being.

This means that everything in this world is like a film being shown on a screen through the projector called *time*.

Being in a state of flux is a part of our very being; the flow of time is woven into the fabric of our existence. The phenomenological world of the third dimension is based on the condition that nothing can ever exist when time is frozen, and nothing can stay the same for more than a moment. Even the cells in your body today are different from the cells you had yesterday. The state of constantly being in flux, this element of flowing time, is part of what allows us to exist right now.

Yet despite this state of flux, there is an aspect of being that is who you are and that gives you your identity, and this aspect of being never changes. Beyond the constant change taking place throughout your physical body, you possess something eternal, an identity that lasts for all time, that philosophers have sometimes referred to as *reality, ideal,* or *idea.* This is true not just for humans, but also for everything around us. There is something in a flower that makes it a flower and not just a random clump of plant cells. If it were truly a random cluster of plant cells, a geranium today might change into an oak tree tomorrow. But a geranium is always a geranium. It will experience change in its natural life cycle, but it will never become an animal or a human being. Nor will it change into a different kind of plant: today's geranium can never be tomorrow's tulip.

In contemplating this aspect of the third dimension, we have found something lasting within the ever-changing, something eternal within the flux. A well-known Buddhist expression, *"matter is void—void is matter,"* articulates the same elusive yet fundamental Truth that I have just explained. Buddhism also teaches that there is something abiding in this world of constant change, and that everything we see as real is merely a projection of something eternal. We are not merely a transient cluster of cells at the complete mercy of time. Beyond the constant flow of life lies an eternal, unchanging aspect of existence. This is our true essence, our reality, our life, our soul, our spirit. By "spirit," I don't mean something ghostly or mysterious, but the very *idea* of life, the reality of the eternal. Spirit is the intelligent individual consciousness that animates the physical body, that governs it and imbues it with existence. This is the specific life force that inhabits every being, whether it is flower or human.

4. The Finite and the Infinite

This discussion of time and existence or reality brings us to the topics of the finite and the infinite which encompass the fields of space and time. Is human life finite or eternal? Does the universe have an end? Or does it extend infinitely? These are questions you may have asked yourself at least once in your life. But before we come to any conclusions, I would like to share with you a story about a turtle.

Once upon a time, there was a huge turtle who lived on a tiny island. Being a turtle, he moved slowly. It took the turtle ten minutes to move each of his legs. One day, this turtle wondered if there was an end to the beach he saw in front of him, so he set out to find out. Summoning all his strength and determination, he began to march along the shoreline. But no matter how far he walked, the beach still extended endlessly ahead. Undeterred, he kept going. Eventually, the exhausted turtle died, but he died proudly, believing he must have explored at least half the world.

The following day, a fisherman found the turtle, carried it to his house on the other side of the island, and cooked it for dinner. It took him less than ten minutes to make the trip. The poor turtle had been walking around and around the sandy beach of this tiny island, never noticing because the waves of the Pacific Ocean had been washing away his footprints.

When I think about the topic of the finite and infinite, I always remember this story. What was the difference between the turtle and the fisherman? There were many differences—how quickly they could walk, the size of their bodies, and the extent of their experiences, for example. But the fundamental difference lay in the levels of their awareness. The turtle's ambitious goal, and the effort and determination with which he pursued it were praiseworthy, but this story is colored by pathos. It points out the undeniable difference between one being who can perceive the truth, and another who cannot.

Now, try replacing the turtle with a person who believes in materialism, and the fisherman with a practitioner of the Truths. Some materialists may be offended, but I dare say that the comparison holds. People who adhere to materialism believe that life lasts only sixty or seventy years and then ends completely in death. They believe only what they can see with their eyes and stoutly deny anything that they can't detect with their five senses. They are like the turtle that set out to explore the world and never noticed that he was merely walking in circles on a tiny island. Unaware that a greater world exists beyond what they can see, both the turtle and the staunch materialist sweat and toil, but fail to live life to the fullest. This is why this story is so sad.

The truth is that long ago, we were given eternal life. Since then, we have reincarnated into this world over and over to fulfill the spiritual training of the soul. The spaces in which our souls live are not limited to this world in the third dimension. Earth's spiritual field is far larger than that; it extends to the tenth dimension. In spirit form, before and after our lives on Earth, we inhabit the spirit world, which begins in the fourth dimension. Where we reside in this system depends on our level of awareness, and wherever we live, we are always surrounded by like-minded companions.

So if you are wondering whether the universe is finite or extends endlessly, you must ask yourself whether you are considering just the three-dimensional universe, or the multidimensional universe that extends beyond the third dimension. If we use the analogy of the human body to understand the greater cosmic universe, then our three-dimensional universe would be the unclothed body. The fourth dimensional universe is equivalent to adding undergarments, the fifth dimension a shirt, and the sixth dimension a sweater. The seventh dimension requires the addition of a suit for men and formal attire for women, and the eighth dimension adds an overcoat. The ninth dimension, finally, would be the hat, which is the highest dimension that Earth's reincarnating souls can live in. This, of course, is just an analogy, but it nicely represents the structure of the multidimensional universe. Just like the example of the human body, higher dimensions layer above lower ones; the dimensions are not completely separate from one another. The higher dimensions envelop the lower dimensions and contribute a higher consciousness and purpose.

5. The Universe Is Multidimensional

The word *dimension* is crucially important to understanding the many worlds that lie beyond this one, and you may be wondering what I mean by it. My definition is similar to common usage, but it's also a bit different. In the context of this book, "dimensions" are ways of describing the characteristics of a specific world and its inhabitants according to how many traits they possess.

For instance, the first dimension is a world made up of straight lines (which themselves are points strung together). If the first dimension had inhabitants, their length would be the only way to distinguish one from another. If two inhabitants were exactly the same length, no one would be able to tell them apart.

The second dimension is a world of length and width, which introduces the existence of a plane. If the second dimension had inhabitants, they would look like paper cutouts. If two people were exactly the same shape and size, they would be indistinguishable.

Then what about the third dimension, the world we inhabit now? This world is composed of three elements that define physical shape and form as we know it: length, width, and height. In the third dimension, two people could only be identical if they shared exactly the same proportions of these three elements. This provides a more sophisticated way of distinguishing one person from another.

In the fourth dimension, the element of time is added to length, width, and height. In our world, things that exist in the same general space will also exist in the same time, but this is not the case in the fourth dimension. When you meet someone here on Earth and shake hands, both of you share the same moment on the same day of the same week in the same year. It is different in the fourth dimension, where two people shaking hands could be living in completely different periods in history. For example, if two Americans were meeting and shaking hands at a specific location, it would be possible for one of them to be from the Colonial period and the other to have lived during the Great Depression. This would never happen in the third dimension, but it happens all the time in the fourth. In the fourth dimension, it is difficult to tell if the building in front of you exists now, or if it stood there centuries ago because even if it were an image from the past, you would still be able to touch it and feel it as if it were real.

In the world of the fourth dimension, everybody's watch shows a different time. You could meet a beautiful woman in her early twenties who lived on Earth in Japan's Heian period (794–1195). The same principle applies to *future* events: inhabitants of the fourth dimension can predict something that will occur in the third dimension's future because for them it would seem as if it were occurring right now.

The fifth dimension introduces the element of spiritual virtue. Its inhabitants are distinct from one another not only in shape and the time period to which they belong, but also in the level of their spiritual awareness. Having spiritual awareness—knowing that we are fundamentally spiritual beings—is a requirement for becoming an inhabitant of this world. This element of spirituality is principally measured by "goodness." Therefore, the fifth dimension is a world filled with virtuous people.

Knowledge of the Truths is the additional element found in the sixth dimension, which means that the inhabitants of this world are different in all the ways of the fifth dimension, as well as in their knowledge of the Truths. The qualifications for living in the sixth dimension are virtue and having learned Buddha's teachings. Of course, the degree of learning varies from person to person. Differences in the level of study determine the finer distinctions that exist within the sixth dimension, but every inhabitant of this dimension believes and trusts in the Truths.

6. The Higher Dimensions of the Universe

Now we move on to the seventh dimension and beyond. In addition to all the qualities of the sixth dimension, the seventh dimension is characterized by the element of altruism. Inhabitants of dimensions below the seventh still live in a very self-focused way, which is not a negative reflection on them, but a simple observation. Even those who live in the sixth dimension, while very advanced, are still striving to absorb as much of the Truths as possible for their own spiritual improvement and growth. They, and all the inhabitants of the dimensions below them, are like students who haven't yet completed their formal education. To extend this analogy, inhabitants of the sixth dimension are like university students, those of the fifth are like high school students, and those in the fourth dimension are like middle school students, while we in the third dimension are in elementary school.

When people are admitted to the seventh dimension, their education is complete; they have become fully aware members of society. In this dimension, their hearts are filled with love toward others, and all their deeds are based on self-less service. Inhabitants of the seventh dimension are always giving love to each other, but they are also actively instructing and guiding residents of lower dimensions, especially the fourth dimension, where inhabitants have not yet fully realized that they are spiritual beings and are in search of salvation through goodness. Finally, some spirits of the seventh dimension choose to reincarnate in human form in the third dimension, so that they may give their love and service for the benefit of all beings living on Earth.

In the eighth dimension, compassion is added to the seven prior elements. Compassion is the desire to give unconditional mercy, and these higher sacred beings offer it freely, without reservation or distinction. While the love of the seventh dimension could be called a "love that gives," the even higher love of the eighth dimension could be described as "love that gives inexhaustibly," or without limit. The love of the seventh dimension can be achieved by human endeavor; the spirits here share with others the love that they themselves have accumulated through effort. In comparison, the love of the eighth dimension is never-ending much like the sun; it is true compassion. Inhabitants of the seventh dimension give their love to specific people and give different amounts of love to different people. By contrast, the love of the eighth dimension is absolutely fair and selfless; it is so magnanimous that it has transcended any human notion of partiality and is given freely to all. It is because they provide all beings with this unlimited love that inhabitants of the eighth dimension deserve to be honored as great leaders.

The framework of the ninth dimension includes a new element I call *cosmic universality*. In the eighth dimension and below, inhabitants live within the multilayered structure of planet Earth's spiritual field. The ninth dimension, however, reaches beyond Earth's spiritual field, connecting it to the spirit worlds of other planets beyond our solar system. So the inhabitants of the ninth dimension guide the Earth's spirit group based on an awareness of and involvement in spiritual evolution on a larger scale, as part of the greater cosmic universe. The deities of world religions, who have been considered the source of the Laws, inhabit this ninth dimension. The only aspect that distinguishes these gods from one another is their unique color of light, each of which is considered the source of the Laws. The Laws themselves ultimately come from one source, Buddha's

Laws, but the different ninth-dimensional spirits express them differently, in seven unique colors.

Beyond the ninth dimension lies the highest level of Earth's spirit group, the tenth dimension. None of the inhabitants in this realm are ever born as humans on Earth; they have no human character. In fact, there are only three spirits in the tenth dimension, who exist as separate consciousnesses. These three inhabitants of the tenth dimension possess the compassion of the eighth dimension and the universality of the ninth, and they also take on roles in *creation* and *evolution*. The sole differences between these three consciousnesses lie in their different responsibilities in the processes of creation and evolution; they no longer have the unique human personalities that are found in lower dimensions.

The three consciousnesses of the tenth dimension are Sun Consciousness, Moon Consciousness, and Earth Consciousness. The Sun Consciousness governs the will of the positive and active forces at work in all living creatures on Earth, including humans. The Moon Consciousness governs the feminine elements of restraint, elegance, and grace. And Earth Consciousness is the life force within the planet itself, responsible for the creation of everything on Earth. The work of these three great planetary consciousnesses has shaped everything that has happened in the 4.6-billion-year history of our planet Earth.

The multidimensional world within Earth's system ends

with the tenth dimension, but beyond that lies the eleventh dimension, which is part of the multidimensional structure of the solar system. The structural element of this eleventh dimension is known as "the mission of the solar system." The life force or spirit body of our sun is an example of eleventh-dimensional existence. Beyond this lies the galactic consciousness of the twelfth dimension, an unfathomably large spirit responsible for our galaxy. This spirit governs countless eleventh-dimensional stellar consciousnesses, including that of our own sun.

It is almost impossible to describe what lies beyond the twelfth dimension in the way that I've done with the worlds that exist within Earth's multidimensional territory, but I can say that the Primordial Buddha of the greater universe, whom we also call Primordial God and is the ultimate spiritual entity, most likely exists beyond the twentieth dimension. In the next section, I will give you a glimpse into the higher worlds of the multidimensional universe that exists beyond our solar system.

7. The Birth of Life (1): The Birth of Stars and Planets

Inquiry into the afterlife—what happens to us after we cease to exist on Earth—is a subject principally discussed in religion, while inquiry into the mysteries of Creation is largely a subject discussed in science. In the sections that follow, I would like to show you that religious inquiry and scientific inquiry are ultimately one and the same, and that they reveal both the mysteries of the birth of life and the truth of Creation.

The cosmic universe's third dimension, of which our planet is a member, is known to have come into existence approximately forty billion years ago. The Primordial Buddha of the cosmic universe, the fundamental God who exists in the twentieth dimension or higher, has existed as a consciousness from time immemorial, and the Creation of the cosmic universe has been part of His mission. Approximately one hundred billion years ago, He had the intention of creating the three-dimensional cosmic universe. Then, about eighty billion years ago, through His Will, He created a Cosmic Spirit who would be in charge of governing the three-dimensional universe. This marked the birth of a spirit of the thirteenth dimension, the very first spirit involved in the universe we see and live in.

This Cosmic Spirit of the thirteenth dimension was created as a projection of the Primordial Buddha's consiousness and approximately 65 billion years ago, the Cosmic Spirit set out to create the galactic consciousnesses of the twelfth dimension, including that of the Milky Way galaxy that we inhabit. In total, as many as two million galactic consciousnesses populate the cosmic universe.

Around sixty billion years ago, the galactic consciousnesses of the twelfth dimension created the stellar consciousnesses of the eleventh dimension. In doing so, they gave form to eleventh-dimensional space for the first time. In our own part of the universe, the twelfth-dimension consciousness of the Milky Way galaxy created the eleventh-dimension consciousness of our sun.

Approximately 53 billion years ago, in the Milky Way galaxy, the stellar consciousnesses of the eleventh dimension began to create planetary consciousnesses, which marked the birth of the tenth dimension. In the solar system of which we are a part, the stellar consciousness of the eleventh dimension (the solar system consciousness) created in succession the planetary consciousnesses of Mercury, Venus, Earth, Mars, Jupiter, Saturn, and the other planets, a process completed around 42 billion years ago.

Approximately forty billion years ago, an extraordinary phenomenon occurred inside the consciousness of the thirteenth dimension's Cosmic Spirit. Massive amounts of nuclear fusion and fission triggered the spectacular cosmic fireworks known as the Big Bang. This phenomenon gave birth to three-dimensional space within the spirit body of the cosmic thirteenth dimension. To use the human body as an analogy, three-dimensional space would be an internal organ of the thirteenth dimension. At first, however, it looked like an enormous cloud floating within space.

In time, the galactic consciousnesses of the twelfth dimension, the stellar consciousnesses of the eleventh dimension, and the planetary consciousnesses of the tenth dimension worked together to create the physical forms of galaxies, nebulae, stars, and planets within the new three-dimensional space, gradually organizing it into the form we see today.

During the forty billion years since the creation of three-dimensional space, the rate of Creation has varied from galaxy to galaxy and from one solar system to another. Our solar system emerged in three-dimensional space approximately ten billion years ago. Mercury was born seven billion years ago, Venus six billion years ago, and Earth about 4.6 billion years ago. That was how the stars and planets, including our own, came into existence, and they were the first consciousnesses to come into physical being in the third dimension.

8. The Birth of Life (2): The Birth of Human Spirits and Other Life Forms

So far, I have been discussing the Creation of the greater universe. But now, I will focus on Earth's solar system, and describe the process of the creation of individual souls. The exact timing of the birth of the first human soul in the greater universe is unclear. However, it is unquestionably true that the three-dimensional universe first took shape forty billion years ago, and that after the arrival of our solar system in the three-dimensional system, planets were born, and various living creatures began to appear on these planets.

The first living creature in our solar system appeared on the planet Venus. Before Venus was created, our Solar System was uninhabitable. Venus first took form six billion years ago, but it would take another half billion years before the ninth-dimensional world of our solar system would be created. When it was created, 5.5 billion years ago, a more active and dynamic spirit than the tenth-dimensional spirit was also created to govern the living creatures that would develop on that planet. This personified form of the consciousness of planet Venus became the very first Grand Spirit of the ninth dimension. He was a spirit advanced to the highest degree. His name was El Miore.

The first experimental creatures that El Miore introduced to the third dimension on Venus were half animal and half plant. Their upper bodies were lilies, they walked on two legs, and a thick growth of leaves covered their backs, supplying them with energy through photosynthesis. Self-sustainability and longevity were two characteristics of this prototypical creature. Next, El Miore separated plants from animals and let them evolve for about two billion years. In their beauty and grace, the plants and animals on Venus differed from those that would later develop on planet Earth.

Venusian plants had jewel-like flowers that perfumed the air with heavenly scents, while the animals were elegant and refined: some could even talk.

Eventually, El Miore created a race of Venusians that more closely resembled the human beings that exist on our planet today. For over one billion years, he continued to refine and recreate these human Venusians as they lived through the rise and fall of countless civilizations. As a result, Venusians advanced to the point of being able to visit other solar systems on spaceships. In their final stage of evolution, Venusians looked like modern earth people but were far more intelligent, possessing IQ's of over 300, and in their pearlescent radiance, Venusians looked more like celestial beings than human beings. Venusian women possessed such beauty that the most beautiful women on Earth would look simian by comparison.

On their planet, the Venusians built a utopian society based on the pursuit of love, wisdom, self-reflection, and progress. When the level of love, beauty, intelligence, and the achievement of ideals developed, and the entire planet reached such heights that it approached the state of the seventh-dimensional World of Bodhisattvas, El Miore received the following message from the Primordial Buddha of the greater universe.

"The experiment with civilization on Venus has been a brilliant success. It has exceeded all expectations. A state of perfect harmony has been achieved, making any further progress impossible. Tragically, a massive volcanic eruption will occur soon, making it difficult for advanced life-forms to survive any longer on this planet. Therefore many of its inhabitants should emigrate to star clusters friendly to Venus, and help in their evolution. The remaining spirits should stay in Venus's spirit world for several hundred thousand years, and the advanced spirits of this group will contribute to the creation of a new spirit group on neighboring Earth. Planet Earth will be a completely blank slate where you will be creating a brand new Utopia. You shall invite foreign souls from unknown stars and educate them, which will contribute to the Milky Way galaxy's evolution."

While Venus was undergoing its experiment with civilization and developing into an advanced planet, the three consciousnesses of the Earth's tenth dimension had been planning the Creation of life on Earth. They decided to build a greater emphasis on dynamic evolution into the structure of Earth's spirit group, because Earth's environment was favorable to this approach. Acting on the advice of El Miore, the three spirits of the tenth dimension—the Sun Consciousness, the Moon Consciousness, and the Earth Consciousness—decided to establish two major principles for life on planet Earth.

The first principle gave diversity to the level of advancement of life forms in the third dimension. It created tiers that established more- and less-advanced creatures. The second

principle was to limit the life span of all creatures and introduce a system of reincarnation that would allow them to live
in cycles between this world and the multidimensional world.
Based on the first principle, simple organisms like amoebas
and plankton were created on our planet approximately three
billion years ago. These became the basis of all animal life.
About 2.6 billion years ago, mold and other fungal growths
were created and became the precursors to vegetable life.
Gradually, increasingly complex life forms were created and
sent to the third dimension.

In accordance with the second principle, the bottom tier
of the spirit world was created first. Although this would later
develop into the fourth-dimensional Posthumous World, at
the time it was not clearly differentiated; it resembled a misty
veil without defined boundaries, hovering above land. Early
microbes and primitive plants reincarnated between the lower
spirit world and the land.

Then, about six hundred million years ago, Earth's three
planetary spirits saw that the time had finally come to introduce superior life forms here. First, they created the Earth's
ninth-dimensional spirit world and invited El Miore from
Venus, the more advanced planet, to direct Earth's development; El Miore became the first ninth-dimensional being in
Earth's spirit group. The Grand Spirit El Miore, the very
first personified spirit on Earth, set out on his first task. He
transferred to Earth the spiritual life forms that he had cre-

ated in the early stages on Venus, and from them, he conceived advanced animals—mainly mammals. How did El Miore go about the task of bringing these advanced animals into creation? First, he used his will to create the consciousnesses of these animals in the lower spirit world. By thinking of the concept, or *idea*, of animals such as mice, rabbits, dogs, and cats, he brought them into being in the lower spirit world. Then, one after another, he materialized these consciousnesses into the third dimension.

In this way, advanced animals began thriving in the third dimension, and the system of reincarnation began to run smoothly. Then, at last, El Miore spoke with the three planetary consciousnesses of the tenth dimension and insisted that the time had come to create humankind onto Earth. Approximately four hundred million years ago, they agreed that the time was right. At this point, El Miore changed his name to El Cantare, which means "the beautiful land of light, Earth." Around 2,500 years ago, part of El Cantare's consciousness took human form and lived in India as Gautama Siddhartha who became known as Shakyamuni Buddha, the founder of Buddhism.

9. The Beginning of Earth's Spirit Group

As we've seen, El Cantare planned planet Earth's spirit group based on two principles. First, he gave humankind varying levels of spiritual awareness to create limitless possibilities for higher evolution. Then, he limited the human lifespan, which encouraged constant reincarnation between the third dimension and the spirit world.

El Cantare set out to create human life forms from the highly developed spirit bodies of Venusians. He amplified his light of compassion and wisdom, generating a massive sphere of light in the ninth dimension. Then, he sent the most highly developed Venusian spirits into it, gave them the power of regeneration, and eventually divided the sphere into hundreds of smaller spheres of light. This is how he created the Guiding Spirits of Light, who belong to Earth's Major Heaven of the eighth and lower dimensions.

To give each of these spirits a personality of its own, El Cantare summoned all the powers of the ninth dimension to materialize them in the third dimension. At first, transparent mirage-like images appeared, which gradually formed into silhouettes that resembled the human form. Finally, shimmering physical bodies emanating white light emerged. El Cantare was delighted by the beauty and excellence of his Creations, as the first five, then ten, then one hundred, then five hundred of these bodies materialized out of thin air.

Next, El Cantare divided these spirits into two groups. He bestowed the light of Venusian wisdom and courage on those to his right, and the light of Venusian beauty and grace to those on his left. In this way men and women came into being. These spirits later became the advanced spirits who are known to us today as Greek gods and goddesses, and Buddhist tathagatas, bodhisattvas, and goddesses.

As their physical descendants multiplied, many of these advanced Venusians accumulated a wealth of experiences as physical beings in the third dimension of Earth. Eventually, when the population in the third dimension reached 770 million, El Cantare felt that humans also needed experience as leaders. He decided to give these advanced humans leadership experiences by giving them a chance to teach and nurture creatures more advanced than primates. So he decided to invite humanoid beings from other stars. He invited three ninth-dimension Grand Spirits from distant constellations to aid him in planning the migration of these beings to our planet. They were Amor (Jesus Christ) from Sagittarius, Therabim (Confucius) from Cygnus, and Moria (Moses) from Cancer.

At this time, however, dinosaurs and other gigantic life forms were beginning to prowl the surface of the Earth. The three ninth-dimension Grand Spirits feared that the new migrants, unused to this hostile environment, would be killed. For this reason, they decided to first invite to Earth the more aggressive, egocentric, and combative humanoids of the Magellanic Clouds. These humanoids possessed highly advanced technology and came to Earth in spacecraft. Physically, they closely resembled people of today, except for their pointy ears and feline tail. Over time, these features gradually disappeared, but when these souls returned to the spirit world, some of them took on the forms of goblins, sorcerers, ogres, monsters, and the like, because their minds, and therefore their self-images, resembled the states of mind possessed by these types of creatures.

The advanced human beings originally created by El Cantare were like the royal family, royal leaders of Earth; they implemented a plan to help the migrants assimilate to life on Earth. However, some leaders among the migrants, while they possessed large amounts of light energy, also behaved like selfish and vengeful gods and disturbed the planet's harmony. Because of their behavior, these immigrants were banished from Major Heaven and were sealed into Minor Heaven. This is how Heaven's sixth, seventh, and eighth dimensions were divided vertically into Major Heaven and Minor Heaven.

Enlil, who resides in the ninth dimension, is one of the leaders of Minor Heaven. One of Enlil's subordinates, Lucifel, was born in the third dimension some 120 million years ago under the name Satan. By becoming enamored with worldly status, fame, material possessions, and sensual pleasures, Lucifel fell from grace. Unable to return to the higher spirit world, he started a revolt and formed the world of Hell in the lowest part of the spirit world. After changing his name to Lucifer, he became king of this new realm.

Because the migrants from the Magellanic Clouds were overly aggressive and lacked harmonious qualities, El Cantare decided to also invite a different type of humanoid race to Earth. So 270 million years ago, the second major migration from outer space took place: one billion beings from the constellation Orion came to Earth in an enormous fleet of space ships. By this time, ten billion of the spirits that El Cantare had originally created from Venusian spirits had experienced incarnations on planet Earth. Their population was large enough to allow for such a massive immigration of new humanoid races. To make room for this influx of souls, the World of Goodness of the fifth dimension was enlarged and prepared for their arrival.

During this mass immigration, three ninth-dimensional Grand Spirits also came to Earth; their names were Achemene, Orgon, and Kaitron. Achemene is Manu, known in Indian mythology as the "progenitor of humankind." Orgon, also known as Maitrayer, was very active during the age of Lamudia and Atlantis, but has rarely incarnated in the third dimension during the last ten thousand years. Kaitron, known in theosophy as Koot Hoomi, is in charge of the development of science and technology. He was born in Greece as Archimedes, and more recently reincarnated in Britain, where he was called Isaac Newton.

Approximately 150 million years ago, the core consciousness of El Cantare incarnated into the third dimension and built a magnificent civilization of light. He established Buddha's Truths for Earth, which greatly advanced the education of the new migrant races. An increasingly vast number of people devoted themselves to El Cantare, creating a common identity, as earth people, that encompassed all souls of Earth.

By continuing the process of splitting light in the higher spirit world, El Cantare continued to increase the size of his spirit group. One hundred thirty million years ago, the number of individual spirits on Earth finally exceeded forty billion. At this memorable moment, a third massive migration took place, as approximately two billion beings from the constellation Pegasus came to Earth. On this occasion, Theoria and Samatria—the ninth and tenth spirits of the ninth dimension—also came to Earth. Theoria was born in Greece some three thousand years ago, and was known as Zeus. Samatria was born twice in the region now known as Iran. He incarnated first as Zoroaster and then as Mani, and founded both Zoroastrianism and Manichaeism.

In this way, ten Grand Spirits assembled in the ninth dimension and became the governing system of Earth's spirit group. Also around this time, the Posthumous World of the fourth dimension was given the role of housing some of the souls that I will be describing in the next section.

10. *The Growth of Earth's Spirit Group and the Origin of Corruption*

By approximately 130 million years ago, the El Cantare spirit group had expanded to more than forty billion souls, while the population of migrant souls totaled more than three billion. It was around this time that Enlil suggested a significant increase in the number of migrant souls from other stars. Enlil proposed using relatively advanced migrant souls as a core, and dividing them to create five more branches of each. According to his idea, if these souls each took turns experiencing life in the third dimension, then soul training would be more efficient.

To divide these souls, Enlil created a gigantic device called a Pytron. The Pytron used amplified light from higher dimensions to irradiate a core spirit, which produced five branch spirits. Several hundred million human spirits were created in this way, but the use of the Pytron was eventually abandoned because so many of the branch spirits produced were spiritually inferior. During their lives in the third dimension, they tended to forget their original nature as souls and became deluded by material things and worldly desires. They exerted an increasingly bad influence on other souls, and after they died, they began to create a spiritual field of their own in the lower realms of the spirit world. As souls with dark thoughts started to gather in the Posthumous World of the fourth dimension, they formed the beginning of Hell.

The Pytron was the second mistake Enlil made, the first being the disharmony created by Enlil's group of migrant souls from the Magellanic Clouds. So once again, he received a stern censure from El Cantare. Moreover, when Lucifer organized a rebellion against the Divine Spirits of Heaven and set up a larger territory of Hell 120 million years ago, the negative thought energy of Hell's inhabitants caused dark clouds to form, cutting off Buddha's light. Never again would His light reach their world and Hell became a cold, dark place. These clouds also had consequences for the third dimension. No matter how brightly the sun might be shining, clouds always create shadows below them. The formation of dark clouds in the fourth dimension blocked His light from shining onto some areas of the third dimension, as well. As a result, for the last 120 million years, the three-dimensional world has been subject to dark storms of negative thoughts that have led to all kinds of evil and chaos.

The conflict between Heaven and Hell has been unfolding for over one hundred million years, and the third dimension has been the center of this battle. Tathagatas and bodhisattvas of the higher echelons of Heaven strive to purify the third dimension, but they have had to fight Lucifer-led demons and evil spirits that try to escape the agonies of Hell by expanding their territory into the third dimension. To solve this problem, El Cantare has sent many fragments of his consciousness to the third dimension on numerous occasions to provide enlightenment. In this way, he has guided and nurtured souls and formed a system that fosters the development of people into Guiding Spirits of Light.

This book, *The Laws of the Sun,* has been written so the sun of Buddha's Truths will regain its brilliance, and His light will once again shine brightly onto the third dimension. I hope that by gaining a deeper understanding of the true history of the Earth's spirit group, you will understand the sincere and earnest hopes that I carry within my heart as I expound the Laws. *The Laws of the Sun* is a book of the Laws that will bring salvation to the world and restore the original world of light—Heaven on Earth.

BUDDHA'S TRUTHS
SPEAK

1. The Truth about the Soul

In chapter I, we explored how the universe was created and how the Earth's spirit group was formed. As we have seen, Creation was a process in which higher-dimension consciousnesses created lower-dimension beings. This all began beyond the twentieth dimension with the Will of the Primordial Buddha, who determined that a succession of grand consciousnesses would inhabit the high dimensions. After stellar consciousnesses and planetary consciousnesses had been created, the Big Bang took place inside the Cosmic Spirit, giving birth to our three-dimensional universe. In time, stars came into existence, and room was made for spirits below the ninth dimension to dwell in each solar system.

In our solar system, the Creation of the Earth's spirit world began with the formation of the Cosmic World of the ninth dimension. The lower dimensions were then created in this order: first, the eighth-dimension World of Tathagatas, then the seventh-dimension World of Bodhisattvas, then the World of Light of the sixth dimension, then the World of Goodness of the fifth dimension, then the Posthumous World of the fourth dimension (which includes both the Astral Realm and Hell). Similar multidimensional structures also exist in other parts of the universe, and Earth's ninth dimension is connected to those spirit worlds. The worlds below the eighth dimension, however, are more bounded, which means that they develop independently of the spirit worlds of other planets.

When we see this structure, it becomes clear that the soul of each individual is a manifestation of the Primordial Buddha on a lower level. This means that He exists not as a separate entity outside you, but as a high consciousness at the very root of your existence. In other words, you are part of His consciousness and therefore an expression of Himself.

The grand universe, and all life forms within it, are manifestations of the Primordial Buddha. They are all projections of His Will. This means that if He were to stop willing us into existence, then in that moment, this seemingly infinite three-dimensional universe that we live in would vanish. Humankind would disappear without a trace. But there's nothing to fear: the fact that you are part of Buddha's consciousness means that your existence is very precious to Him.

Delight in the fact that you are part of Buddha! Take pride in being a facet of His self-expression. This is the Truth about souls, and leaders throughout history have developed various religions and philosophies to awaken people to this Truth. Revealing this Truth is the ultimate purpose of all the sciences, which have made tremendous strides in recent years. Keeping in mind the glorious Truth that you are part of Buddha's consciousness, let's take a look at the soul itself. For when we discover the ideal state of the human soul, Buddha's Truths will be revealed to us.

2. *The Nature of the Soul*

If our souls are part of Buddha, then what does that tell us about the nature of the soul? By exploring the characteristics of the soul, we should be able to catch a glimpse of His nature. The soul has several distinctive qualities. First, the soul is endowed with the creative power to transform itself freely according to its own will. In other words, you have the power to become whatever type of consciousness you would like to be, and to act accordingly. For instance, you could choose to manifest the highest possible degree of love, or you could exercise the highest possible degree of freedom. With your own will, you can control the amount of light that exists within you. You have the power to increase your light and become a higher being, or to reduce your light and inhabit a lower dimension.

So is it because of our soul's creative nature that we humans create Hell and fall into it? Are evil and corruption part of the soul's nature? The answer to these questions is both yes and no. "Yes" because the soul has been granted total freedom to create what it wishes; it has no restrictions or constraints. (And as we know, with freedom comes responsibility.) "No" because the soul itself did not originally contain evil. Evil is simply a distortion caused by conflict between souls that are each acting according to free will. We cannot perpetrate evil when we are all alone. Evil comes into existence only when we come in contact with another person, another creature, or another object. The issue of dualism, of whether good and evil exist independently, has been debated throughout history as people have wondered, "Why does evil exist in a world created by Buddha?" Evil is not part of His divine nature, nor is it a fundamental characteristic of the soul. Evil is a temporary impediment to His Will, friction caused by the workings of the mind, and by the actions that people, in their freedom, choose to take.

The second major characteristic of the soul is that it can absorb and disperse the light of Buddha. But what exactly is this light? It is the boundless energy that fills the universe.

Just as the sun shines on our physical world, Buddha provides massive amounts of energy to the multidimensional universe. No living creature can survive on Earth without the thermal energy that the sun provides, and in the same way, no spiritual being can exist in the spirit world without the light and energy of Buddha.

The soul has the ability to focus, absorb, emit, and amplify the light of Buddha. Those who can absorb and emit a large amount of this light are known as Guiding Spirits of Light. These Guiding Spirits of Light are the tathagatas of the eighth dimension (sometimes referred to as archangels) and the bodhisattvas of the seventh dimension (equivalent to angels). They have the power to concentrate and emanate vast quantities of Buddha's light and to share this light with other people. In other words, they can brighten up another person's heart. So all living souls absorb and emit Buddha's light, but the Guiding Spirits of Light can spread the light, and in so doing, can bring hope to people and create a brighter world.

If all souls have the ability to absorb and emit Buddha's light, what about souls in the realms of Hell? Are they also being supplied the energy of this light? Yes, they are, but souls in Hell are themselves blocking the light with dark clouds of negative energy generated by their negative thoughts. It is as if they are living in a dark cave of their own making. Since their lives are no longer sustained by Buddha's energy, they turn instead to the negative thoughts harbored by people living on Earth.* Spirits in Hell can come into the ordinary world of the third dimension, "plug into" people's minds, and absorb energy from their dark, clouded thoughts. Spirits in Hell are like vampires that suck the energy out of living people and eventually lead them to destruction. If we don't want this to happen, we have to get rid of the negative thoughts that attract and nourish evil spirits. We have to stop creating "mental tumors" that block Buddha's light; instead we need to let this light fill our hearts. When all of us can do this, the inhabitants of Hell will be deprived of their energy supply, and Hell will eventually cease to exist.

3. The Incarnations of Buddha's Light

I would now like to talk about Divine Spirits. The word *angel* has distinctly Christian overtones, while the word *bodhisattva* has Buddhist connotations. However, their meanings are similar. Buddha's Truths are expressed in the teachings of both Christianity and Buddhism; they only seem to be different religions because their founders and the colors of spiritual

---

* People on Earth absorb spiritual energy from Buddha's light to sustain their spiritual lives, just as they consume food and convert it into energy to sustain their physical lives. In a way, humans are like independent power generators.

light that they represent are different. Both Guiding Spirits of Light and Angels of Light are Divine Spirits that reside in higher dimensions of Heaven. In the eyes of ordinary souls, all Divine Spirits are incarnations of Buddha's light.

But why do they exist? If all humans are created equal, then isn't the very existence of these Divine Spirits an act of discrimination against those who dwell in lower dimensions? Doesn't it imply that ordinary people are intended to live ordinary lives forever, while Divine Spirits will always lead a life of nobility? To answer these questions, I must first explain Buddha's view of the world, which is based on two principles: equality and fairness.

All things—human, animal, plant, and mineral—have a fundamentally divine nature. Regardless of outward appearances, everything in Creation is a manifestation of the Will of Buddha. This is the absolute Truth. In other words, all forms of existence are diamonds of His wisdom. To let humans be humans and plants be plants, Buddha sprinkled these diamonds of wisdom and encouraged them to produce unique, vivid expressions and various beautiful shapes. So everything consists of His diamonds of wisdom. This is the Truth.

Buddhism calls these diamonds "Buddha-nature," and teaches that all living beings possess them, for we are all children of Buddha. In this respect, all beings *are* equal, whether they reside in higher dimensions or lower: they are all manifestations of His energy. But people are often misled by the words "higher" and "lower."

There are basically three kinds of spirits: highly developed spirits, developing spirits, and undeveloped spirits. All spirits are walking the same path, but the difference is in the distance they have traveled. Some are walking farther ahead, while others are walking further behind. Most Guiding Spirits of Light, highly advanced spirits, are very ancient souls, so they have already walked a great distance and are therefore much closer to reaching the state of Buddha. Most undeveloped souls are newer, so they are naturally walking behind, having only recently set out on the path.

You probably would not consider it unfair to assess them based on the distance they have traveled. So souls can be equal and still exist at different levels; it simply means that they have traveled different distances. Even old souls do not necessarily advance in the right direction; some who were once angels have fallen to Hell and become devils. Although these souls once made great progress, at some point they decided to turn back the way they came instead of going forward. They should be called regressive spirits rather than undeveloped spirits.

Buddha keeps His promise to provide *equality* by having all souls travel the one path that leads to Him. At the same time, He also keeps His promise to treat all beings *fairly* by allowing them to advance based on the distance they have progressed. Divine Spirits, regarded as incarnations of Buddha's light, have been assigned a role that is appropriate based on their past achievements. All spirits have this in common: they are all eternal travelers who are undergoing spiritual training designed to improve their souls and to help them become Divine Spirits.

4. The Structures of the Soul

Now that we've seen that human souls are in different stages of development, and that Buddha sees this world in terms of both equality and fairness, I would like to share with you my understanding of the structure of the soul. The soul of a person living on Earth is only a small part of his or her larger soul, and we are only aware of the surface consciousness of the soul. The rest of the soul, the subconscious, exists in the spirit world. To help you better understand this idea, let's look more closely at the nature of the soul.

As we saw in chapter I, in the beginning, the Primordial Buddha created the consciousness of the Cosmic Spirit of the thirteenth dimension. This spirit then created the galactic consciousnesses of the twelfth dimension, which then produced the stellar consciousnesses of the eleventh dimension. The stellar consciousnesses then created the planetary consciousnesses of the tenth dimension, which in turn produced the consciousnesses of the ninth dimension, which have human personalities.

The ninth dimension's Grand Spirits therefore have personal characteristics. However, because their energy is too massive to dwell in a single human body, when they incarnate in the three-dimensional material world, they use only a portion of their consciousness. In the cases of Gautama Siddhartha and Jesus Christ, ninth-dimension spirits individuated small portions of their massive energy in human form, thereby creating unique human souls. Grand Spirits of the ninth dimension are capable of splitting themselves into an infinite number of souls, each of which can serve different purposes for the creation of a new civilization. Then when those souls leave the human body and return to the world of the ninth dimension, they become part of the memory of their Grand Spirits.

The situation differs slightly for Great Guiding Spirits of Light in the World of Tathagatas. These spirits of the eighth dimension are also advanced spirits, but their personalities are more distinctive and unique. Eighth-dimension spirits usually live in Heaven as part of one integrated consciousness, but when necessary, they can divide themselves into any number of spirits to achieve a specific purpose. For instance, Yakushi Nyorai, a tathagata of medicine, has one integrated personality as an eighth dimensional spirit. But when help and guidance are needed in the medical arena, he can split his spiritual light to create thousands of spirits, or even tens of thousands, who can then provide medical guidance to other spirits and people all around the world. While Grand Spirits of the ninth dimension can split into independent spirits to achieve a variety of different purposes, eighth-dimension spirits focus on a specific purpose no matter how many spirits they divide into; this is the difference between spirits of the ninth dimension and spirits of the eighth.

Spirits in the World of Bodhisattvas of the seventh dimension have even more individualized human characteristics. Some consciousnesses in the eighth dimension and above have never incarnated on Earth, but all seventh-dimension spirits have experienced life on Earth. The seventh dimension spirits that belong to the El Cantare spirit group place great importance on teamwork, and as a general rule, they form groups of six spirits. The leader of such a group is regarded as the "core spirit," and the other five members are "branch spirits." All six spirits have the same tendencies and similar characteristics, and just as a human body consists of six body parts—a head, two arms, a torso, and two legs—the seventh dimension teams of six spirits make up one integrated soul. These six spirits take turns being born into this world to accomplish their mission of saving people. Experience that any one spirit gains on Earth is shared with the other five spirits. Usually, the spirit who is next in line to be born acts as the guardian of the spirit ahead of it, who has already been born on Earth. Nowadays, however, in order to cope with the complex structure of society, the spirit with the most recent incarnation often takes the role of the guardian spirit so that it can provide guidance based on the very latest information.

In the World of Light of the sixth dimension, however, spirits have little awareness of belonging to a group. Since each spirit acts independently, it has difficulty understanding the concept of soul siblings, or of a core spirit and branch spirits. In the sixth dimension and the worlds below it, there are spirits who were created around one hundred million years ago by a giant device called a Pytron, which magnified the high dimensional light and produced five copies, or branch spirits, of a core sixth-dimension spirit. Because the spiritual awareness of these new copy spirits was lower than that of the original sixth-dimension spirit, most of them became inhabitants of the World of Goodness of the fifth dimension and the Posthumous World of the fourth dimension. In order to raise their spiritual level, these copy spirits reincarnate quite frequently, moving between our three-dimensional material world and the spirit world.

In the sixth dimension and below, the core spirit usually protects and guides its branch spirits when they are born on Earth to undergo soul training. Sometimes, however, as a result of their different experiences on Earth, a disparity develops between the awarenesses of the six spirits. If this disparity becomes too great, then it can become difficult to keep the same team of six spirits together. In such cases, they receive the power of Buddha's light to form new groups with different spirits.

5. The System of Guardian Spirits and Guiding Spirits

In the world of religion, people often use the terms *guardian spirits* and *Guiding Spirits*. I would like to explain these terms, beginning with *guardian spirit*. People often believe that everyone has a guardian spirit, and that if the guardian spirit is strong, that person's life will improve, but if the guardian spirit is weak, that person will experience misfortune. Guardian spirits do indeed exist. Everyone has one, and your guardian spirit can influence your life to a certain extent. But the important question is, why do these guardian spirits, who reside in the spirit world, protect humans living on Earth? It is time now for this secret to be revealed.

More than three hundred million years ago, when highly advanced humans of the El Cantare spirit group first began to live on Earth, they did not have guardian spirits. In those days, people's hearts were so pure that they were able to communicate directly with the spirit world while they lived on Earth. Hell did not exist, so there were no evil spirits, which meant that it was unnecessary to assign guardian spirits to protect humans from negative influences. About 120 million years ago, however, spirits with unharmonious vibrations began to gather in the Posthumous World of the fourth dimension, the lowest level of Heaven. These spirits gradually created the dark realm of Hell. No longer able to receive energy from Buddha's light, these spirits began to feed on the negative energy of people on Earth. To ensure a steady supply of negative energy, they created confusion on Earth and tempted people until they fell prey to desire, anger, and conflict; harbored evil thoughts such as jealousy, doubts and discontent; and spread disharmony. These evil spirits from Hell plotted to throw the world into complete chaos and to fill people's hearts with distrust.

This situation took the Guiding Spirits of Light by surprise, so they held an emergency meeting in Heaven and discussed how to resolve this problem. They decided to enact a plan suggested by Amor, also known as Jesus Christ. He proposed the following three general rules:

1. To avoid being completely controlled by evil spirits, humans on Earth should no longer be able to communicate directly with the spirit world. Instead, they should be encouraged to make choices that would lead to virtuous lives in the material world.

2. To protect humans from the temptations of Hell, all

spirits should be assigned a guardian spirit when they incarnate on Earth.

3. To prevent people from completely forgetting about the spirit world, Great Guiding Spirits of Light should be sent to Earth at regular intervals to give religious teachings and to increase awareness of the existence of the spirit world.

These three basic rules have been observed for more than one hundred million years. In the meantime, however, Hell expanded its original domain, making it difficult for a single guardian spirit to adequately protect a person undergoing soul training on Earth. And because humans on Earth could no longer have direct communication with the spirit world (unless they were religious or spiritual leaders with psychic abilities), they could not recall their past-life memories; as a result, people forgot their spirituality and became caught up in materialistic desires. To make matters worse, when Guiding Spirits of Light descended to Earth to establish new religions in accordance with the third rule, religious wars and conflict broke out between different sects. Satan and other devils took advantage of this weakness by sneaking into the minds of religious leaders and encouraging them to lead their followers astray. This created further confusion and chaos on Earth.

This situation reveals the importance and the urgency of

our mission to spread Buddha's Truths. It also created the need to modify the second rule, the assignment of guardian spirits. As a rule of thumb, your guardian spirit is either a spirit that split off from your soul, or a spirit that belongs to a group of six that consists of five branch spirits and a core spirit. In addition, if a person on Earth has a critically important mission to accomplish, he or she will be provided with a Guiding Spirit who specializes in that person's particular field. Religious leaders, in particular, are assigned a guide, such as a tathagata or bodhisattva, who possesses a higher spiritual awareness than they themselves possess. In this way, the system of guardian spirits and Guiding Spirits has become stronger; nonetheless, people on Earth are still heavily influenced and misled by various evil spirits.

6. The Evolution of the Soul

Due to the negative influence of Hell, this physical world of the third dimension has experienced great disorder and confusion for the past one hundred million years. But this is not to say that the Earth's spirit group has been stymied in its evolutionary mission. In fact, quite remarkable progress has been made. Among the souls created on Earth, there are distinguished souls who have evolved considerably. Through repeated cycles of reincarnation, they have advanced from the fourth dimension to the fifth, from the fifth to the sixth, and from the sixth to the seventh, reaching the level of Divine Spirits who originally came from other planets. Although none of the spirits created on Earth has yet become a ninth-dimension spirit, some have reached the World of Tathagatas in the eighth dimension. The Grand Spirits of the higher dimensions are delighted by such remarkable progress. This is exactly what they were aiming to achieve when they first formed Earth's spirit group. They emigrated to Earth filled with the hope that they could make Earth more advanced and more harmonious than the planet that they had come from—and now their hopes are coming to pass.

Today, the population of the World of Tathagatas in the eighth dimension is estimated to be about five hundred spirits, and the seventh-dimension World of Bodhisattvas consists of roughly nineteen thousand spirits. Of these, 130 spirits have become tathagatas on Earth, and seven thousand have become bodhisattvas on Earth. Quite a number of new souls created through the Pytron have also managed to prog-ress to the upper realms of the sixth and seventh dimensions. So, while there are sad reports of the expansion of Hell, there is also wonderful news.

Why are souls expected to evolve, and how do they actu-ally do so? To answer the first question, once again we need to track back to the beginning and consider why Buddha cre-ated souls of different levels in the first place. Since He had already achieved the highest level of evolution, there was no need for Him to create souls in lower dimensions and have them evolve for His sake. Buddha created souls, or consciousnesses, of different levels not for the sake of evolution itself, but for the gratification that both He and we can find in that process. Why do parents go through all the effort of having and raising children? Not because parents want to make their children fully developed adults, but because they find joy in the process of raising children. By having children, parents expand their own feelings of happiness. He created souls, or consciousnesses, of various levels because the process of encouraging them to evolve and develop became an expression of His joy and a source of His happiness. This is the fundamental basis of the laws of evolution in the universe. With boundless love, Buddha watches over the countless souls He created as they strive to become closer to Him.

One indication of how much a soul has evolved is the amount of light it emits. The same is true of people on Earth. As they progress spiritually, their inner light increases and their auras begin to glow. Those with spiritual insight can easily determine another person's level of enlightenment. People whose minds are attuned to Hell have a dim aura and have whitish spiritual spots that indicate the body parts that are negatively influenced by spirits from Hell. Those whose minds are connected to the Astral Realm in the fourth dimension have a small aura of just one or two centimeters (half an inch). Those whose minds are attuned to the World of Goodness in the fifth dimension have a slightly larger aura of about three to four centimeters (1.5 inches), and those connected to the sixth-dimension World of Light, have a more powerful circular aura that extends about ten centimeters (four inches). Those who reach the level of an *arhat*, or saint, in the upper levels of the sixth dimension, emit an aura that resembles a small, circular tray of golden light. Those whose minds are attuned to the World of Bodhisattvas of the seventh dimension have a circular golden aura that has grown to forty or fifty centimeters wide (about 1.5 feet). Those whose minds are connected to the World of Tathaga-tas in the eighth dimension have an aura of one to two meters (three to six feet), which lights up their surroundings.

The level of the soul's development can be measured by the light that it emits; in other words, your soul develops when you expand your capacity to receive and hold the light of Buddha. Make diligent efforts to receive as much light as possible, and try not to create dark clouds in your mind that could block His light.

7. The Relationship Between Mind and Soul

Throughout this book I use the terms *consciousness*, *spirit*, and *soul*. Although these terms can be used somewhat interchangeably, it's important to note that the soul has more human attributes than the spirit, and the spirit has more human qualities than consciousness. So what about the mind? Is it the same as the soul? Just as the physical heart acts as the core of the human body, the mind acts as the center of the soul. The mind is not the brain or its cells, which is confirmed by the fact that even after we die and return to the spirit world, we retain every memory from our lives on Earth. The physical body that we leave behind will eventually disappear from this world, but the soul and its core aspect, the mind, can still think, feel, and remember.

The brain simply functions as a control center, where all kinds of information are organized and stored. When this control center is damaged, its commands cannot reach other parts of the body, so we can no longer act normally. In the case of a man who is mentally impaired due to brain injury, his family may think that he is incapable of understanding their words, but this is not true. His mind—the center of his soul—understands, but he cannot communicate this because of the brain injury. However, as soon as he leaves his physical body and returns to the other world, he will regain the ability to fully and freely express himself.

If the mind does not exist in the brain, then is it located in the heart? When we are in shock, our hearts begin to race. When we grieve, our hearts ache. When we are scared, our hearts freeze. When we are happy, our hearts feel warm, and when we are sad, our hearts feel heavy. So the heart is very closely related to the mind, and it is an organ that is susceptible to spiritual influences. However, the physical heart is not the mind itself.

In its original state, a spirit is formless energy. However, that spirit creates energy in a human shape that is called a soul, which has a mind at its center. When the soul dwells in a physical body, the mind's core is situated in the same area as the physical heart, and mainly controls our intentions, emotions, and instincts. The mind also controls intellect and logic, and transmits commands through its control center, the brain. Another part of the soul, which controls spiritual wisdom, runs from the lower belly through the heart and the brain, and is spiritually connected to soul siblings in the spirit world.

Those who lead a materialistic life may deny the existence of the spirit or the soul, but they probably accept the existence of the mind. They may claim that the mind is no more than a function of the brain, but even these people will weep when they are sad without making a conscious decision to do so. The brain does not tell them to cry. When we feel sad, grief fills our hearts in an instant, and tears begin to flow. When we meet an old friend unexpectedly, we feel a surge of joy in our hearts and spontaneously hug that person. These are not the logical reactions of the cerebrum, but reactions of the mind based on our spiritual intuitions. Cerebralism, which states that all psychic phenomena are merely products of the brain, is another form of materialism, which we must dismiss; it is simply wrong.

8. How the Mind Functions

As I have explained, human beings are consciousness, spirits and souls that are created by the Will of Buddha, and at the core of the soul is the mind. Now I would like to further explore what the mind is and how it functions.

It often seems that we can sense other people's thoughts and feelings. For example, when you are attracted to someone, that person seems to somehow sense your feeling, and gradually begins to like you as well. The opposite is also true. When you dislike somebody, that person will often sense your feeling and withdraw from you. How is this kind of telepathic communication possible?

The functions of the mind are creative abilities given to us by Buddha. He created, with His Will, the multidimensional structure of the spirit world, our souls, and our physical bodies. While every human being is a fragment of Buddha's consciousness, each of us is also a complete microcosm. This means that the human mind functions in the same way as His creative power. Every thought we have in our mind actually creates something in the multidimensional universe. Our combined thoughts become the driving force of the spirit world.

Let me add that there are different levels of thinking. First, there are the *thoughts* that come in and out of our minds during the day; these are part of our normal mental activity. The second level, *concepts*, is more concrete. While the first kind of thinking is like waves at the seashore, the second is more consistent and structured; it has a story line and can be visualized. Like the flowing water of a river, it is constant and has a particular direction. The third type of thinking is exertion of the *will*. The will is creative and pursues clear objectives. But beyond this, the will actually possesses a physical force, known as psychokinesis (PK). In the fourth dimension and above, the will has a power similar in kind to Buddha's creative power, and it creates all sorts of things. Even in the three-dimensional world, the mental function of will has great physical power.

For example, if you strongly wish to guide someone in a positive direction, your will may cause a sudden change in that person's mental state, or it may influence their circumstances for the better. If, on the other hand, you have an intense dislike for someone, and this hatred becomes stronger and more focused until it becomes your will, then the recipient might fall ill, experience various misfortunes, or even die young. A similar effect occurs in large groups. If tens of thousands or millions of people strongly wish to make this world a Utopia, their focused and amplified will will shed a ray of light in one corner of the world. This light will then brighten up people's hearts, and happiness will start to spread all over the world, turning it into a world of angels, or Heaven on Earth. Of course, the opposite scenario is also possible. What would happen if this world were full of people with negative thoughts, such as hatred, anger, and self-ishness? Seen with a spiritual eye, this negative energy would look like black thunderclouds floating into different parts of the world and wreaking havoc. The human mind has the amazing power to either create miracles or trigger disasters. This is why we need to be so careful to understand what is on our minds and how the mind functions.

9. The Mind Can Attune to Three Thousand Worlds

Up to this point, I have been describing the power of the mind and how its *thoughts* gain more power as they develop into *concepts* and then into *will*. Now, I would like to take this idea a step further and explain the principle that "the mind can attune to three thousand worlds,"[4] which was taught by the Chinese Buddhist monk T'ien-t'ai Chih-i (537-597) more than a thousand years ago, atop the Tientai Mountains in China. At that time, I was guiding him from Heaven. The teachings I was giving him from the world of the ninth dimension were as follows.

"Everyone has a compass needle of thoughts within their mind. This needle swings constantly and points in various directions all day long. It never knows any rest. Even monks who have devoted their lives to spiritual discipline do not know peace. If a beautiful woman walks by, the needle in a monk's mind swings wildly. If a monk sees a delicious meal, the needle moves again. If a monk sees others advancing in their spiritual awakening, the needle veers off once more. If a monk's master admonishes him, the needle jumps again. In this way, monks' minds know no peace.

"True enlightenment is found in a state of complete harmony and peace, not in a state of constant turmoil. T'ien-t'ai Chih-i, you must gain a deep understanding of this Truth and teach the needle of the mind to point in one direction, the right direction. People will never attain peace of mind as long as the compass needle of their mind remains in motion. In the same way that an ordinary compass needle always points north, so should the needle of the mind always point in the direction of Buddha. Just as the North Star shines in the sky to guide people at night, T'ien-t'ai Chih-i, you must teach people to live with the Will of Buddha as their own. This is the true meaning of having an unshakable mind; it is also what it means to have faith in Buddha.

"The mind is truly mysterious, yet it points the way forward. If your mind is filled with anger, you will be attuned to the Ashura Realm in Hell (the Hell of Strife), and before you know it, your life will be full of destruction. If your mind becomes fixated on sexual pleasure, you will become an instrument of spirits in the Hell of Lust. Even those who seek Buddha on the path to spiritual awakening may find the needle of their mind pointing in the wrong direction. If they become arrogant and boastful, they will mistake the voices of devils for the voices of tathagatas and bodhisattvas. Then they will mislead people with lies instead of truth, and fall into the Abysmal Hell as a result.

"If, on the other hand, your mind is always filled with good thoughts, the needle of your mind will be attuned to the World of Goodness of the fifth dimension. Your friends and ancestors in Heaven will watch over you with a smile. If you devote yourself to helping others, remain humble and modest, and continue to seek the path toward Buddha, your mind will connect to the World of Bodhisattvas of the seventh dimension, and you will become a living angel on Earth.

"There are those whose minds are firmly focused on spreading the Truths. They teach the Truths with a pure heart, and their lives serve as models for all people. Their minds are already connected to the World of Tathagatas of the eighth dimension, and they receive constant guidance from tathagatas in Heaven. The needle of the mind indeed moves in wondrous ways. T'ien-t'ai Chih-i, you must deepen your understanding of this Truth and help others who are undergoing their spiritual training on Earth.

"Heaven and Hell do not only exist in the other world; they also exist here and now. They exist in your mind. The needle of your mind can point in all directions, and depending on your thoughts, you can immediately attune to Heaven or to Hell. This is the teaching of 'the mind can attune to three thousand worlds.' Once people become aware of this Truth, they will want to set aside some time every day to calm their minds, enter a meditative state, look back on their day, reflect on their lives, and correct their wrong thoughts and actions.

"T'ien-t'ai Chih-i, the Noble Eightfold Path that I taught in India was based on this law that I have just now revealed to you. Heaven and Hell exist in the minds of people living in the material world, and their thoughts and the state of their minds in the material world will determine their destinations in the next. This is why human beings must live their lives based on the Eightfold Path.

"The Noble Eightfold Path is composed of the following: Right View, Right Thought, Right Speech, Right Action, Right Livelihood, Right Effort, Right Mindfulness, and Right Concentration.* Only when people have mastered these

---

*The common names of the paths have been used here. *Buddha's Teaching: The Dharma of the Right Mind* (the main sutra for Happy Science members) uses different names, but both versions essentially mean the same thing.

eight principles can they maintain the right state of mind and reach human perfection. T'ien-t'ai Chih-i, correct your thoughts and deeds based on the Eightfold Path, and spread this teaching—that the mind can attune to three thousand worlds. This shall lead to your enlightenment and to enlightenment for the people of the world."

10. Buddha's Teaching: The Eightfold Path

Having explored the concept of "the mind can attune to three thousand worlds," and having touched upon the Noble Eightfold Path, I would like to conclude this chapter by explaining the significance of the Eightfold Path in the context of modern life.

Human beings in this physical world are spiritually blindfolded. We search for a way to survive based solely on information from our five senses, and we often remain unaware of the world that exists beyond them. Although this may seem paradoxical, our five senses help us awaken to that world, because by carefully observing the world around us, we can find evidence that the spirit world exists. We can only find the purpose and meaning of our life on Earth when we discover what lies beyond our five senses. Instead of simply lamenting the fact that we are blind to the Truths of life, we must strive to sharpen our five senses and discover the

Truths. Through this effort, you will discover the essence of the Eightfold Path, the wisdom that shows us the right path and guides us to human perfection.

That said, there is no single answer to the question of how you should live your life. Life presents you with a series of questions that depend on the circumstances you are in, the experience and knowledge you have gained, and the habits you have acquired. Therefore, no one can address these questions but you. If you stray from the correct path, it is your responsibility to find your way back. No one can do that for you, either. This is why each and every one of us must uncompromisingly seek what is right within the framework of our own life. What, then, is the standard for this righteousness? What defines righteousness? It is my mission as a true religious leader to answer this question in this lifetime.

To know what is right is to know the Will of Buddha. His Will establishes what is good and what is evil. His Will determines what is true and what is false. His Will rules what is beautiful and what is ugly. To know His Will is to conduct a scientific inquiry into His life—into the nature of Buddha's light. It is to make the utmost effort to understand Him.

I have written numerous books to help deepen your understanding of the nature of this vast energy that is the Will of Buddha. It is my sincere wish that by understanding my teachings, you will grasp the true meaning of righteousness and use this wisdom as a guide to practice the Eightfold Path. My teachings are Buddha's Truths, and as such, they will deeply touch your soul, and tears of repentance will well up. I invite you to use my teachings as guidelines for living a life of Truth, and to ask yourself the following questions when you reflect on the day's thoughts and deeds.

I. Right View

Did you look at things the way they are, rightly, based on right faith? Did you observe others rightly? Did you treat others with a compassionate heart, in the way that Buddha would treat them? Did you humbly accept His perspective on life and the world?

2. Right Thought

Did you think rightly? Is your aspiration for enlightenment appropriate? Did you harbor any negative thoughts in your mind, such as greed, anger, and discontent? Did you think badly of others, or bear malice toward them? Did you become arrogant or doubt Buddha's Truths? Did you have any thoughts that went against Buddha's Truths? Did you make right judgments?

3. Right Speech

Did you speak rightly? Did you use truthful words? Did you say anything that bothers your conscience? Did you hurt others by using abusive words? Did you lie about the level of your enlightenment, or otherwise use false speech? Did you mislead others by using flattery, or cause others distress by speaking in a way that created distrust between them?

4. Right Action

Did you act rightly? Did you violate any of the precepts for seekers? Did your hands, your legs, or any other part of your physical body commit any crimes, such as murder, assault, and theft? Did you get involved in any sexually immoral acts, such as extramarital affairs, sexual abuse, prostitution, or an obsession with pornography? Did you respect the lives of all living creatures? Did you make generous and sincere offerings to Buddha, Dharma, and Sangha?

5. Right Livelihood

Did you live rightly, keeping your actions, speech, and thoughts in harmony? Did you become obsessed with alcohol, tobacco, gambling, or drugs? Did you have any complaints about your life, or did you know how to be content? Did you give thanks for all things? Did you make full use of the twenty-four hours that were given to you?

6. Right Effort

Did you study the teachings of the Truths in the right way? Did your aspiration for enlightenment remain strong? Did you refrain from doing evil? How many seeds of goodness did you plant? Did you make a constant effort to improve yourself?

7. Right Mindfulness

Were you able to calm your mind to make a right plan to improve your soul and use your life for the creation of Heaven on Earth? Are your prayers for self-realization in accordance with the Will of Buddha, and do they help raise the level of your enlightenment and further refine your character? Do you have a deep understanding of Buddha's Truths? Do you remember the teachings of the Truths correctly?

8. Right Concentration

Did you regularly take time for right meditation? Did you engage in introspection about the sins you've committed in the past? At the end of the day, did you look back over your day thoroughly? Did you feel gratitude toward your guardian spirit and Guiding Spirits? Were you able to attain peace of mind through the practice of meditation?

The Eightfold Path outlined above has its origins in the distant past but has not lost any of its value today.* It teaches us the right way to live. The daily effort of correcting your way of life will make you an extraordinary person and will elevate you toward Buddha.

---

* I explained the Eightfold Path in the same order as originally taught by Shakyamuni Buddha, but in chapter 3, I introduce a different approach, in an effort to make it easier for beginners to put this into practice.

THE RIVER OF
GOD'S LOVE

1. What Is Love?

I invite you to join me in a meditation on the essence of love. Love is undoubtedly the most precious, splendid, and desirable aspect of life. People are intrigued by the word *love*, drawn by the very sound of it. The word *love* puts us in touch with our dreams and ideals. It infuses us with passion for life. It fires the imagination and our greatest aspirations. If you knew that you were destined to die tonight but discovered that someone you care about loves you, you would make the journey to the next world with a blissful smile. A life without love is like an exhausting journey across an endless desert, but bring love to it, and countless flowered oases spring up along the way.

But what exactly *is* love? Have poets, novelists, or philosophers succeeded in defining it? Have religious leaders offered a description that gets to the essence of love? How much do you, yourself, understand love? How deeply have you penetrated its true nature? God gave humankind this question about the nature of love as a challenge for us to answer. Taking on that challenge can be profoundly joyful, but it can also cause us suffering.

As we contemplate this question, we see that love has extremes. At one end, true love fills us to the brim with happiness; at the other, a false form of love plunges us into the deepest despair. The majority of the happiness we experience in life comes from love; at the same time, love also makes up the majority of life's distresses when we misunderstand it. But there is hope; there is a way to conquer false love in our pursuit of the greatest happiness achievable. If we can understand what love is in its purest form and become masters of the art of giving love, then a ray of hope will be shining at the end of our quest. God awaits us at our destination, with His benevolent smile and open arms.

In this chapter, I describe the nature of true love, its different stages, the relationship between love and enlightenment, and finally, the connection between God and love. Jesus Christ is one of the greatest envoys of God's love that the world has ever known. He is true champion of the subject. He says with a tremendous sense of urgency that we must spread a higher awareness of love's true form to people of the modern age. I have had and continue to hold many conversations about love with Jesus Christ, who is in Heaven. According to him, love has never been as misunderstood as it is today; the age that led to the destruction of Atlantis and the period culminating in the end of Sodom and Gomorrah are among the only periods in history that compare to what we face today.

I hope to take on this topic of love myself, and tackle its most difficult questions. I would like to help untangle the misperceptions about love that are prevalent today, and offer you an extensive meditation on the subject. What people need to do most is study love as they practice the Eightfold Path as their discipline. These practices are blessings that shall become the new gospel for people living today. Join me in this chapter as I set out to provide you with a new perspective on life, the world, and the Truths, by seeing them through the lens of love.

2. Love Exists

All of us have had many opportunities to contemplate love, yet none of us has ever seen it. We cannot hold love in our hands or take it out and show it to people. However, no one has ever doubted that love exists. We all believe that it does, and we seek more of it. We all set out on the eternal journey through life with this aspiration for a love that we can be sure of.

If no one has ever seen or touched love, could it be just a fantasy? When we consider this, we find that love is not the only invisible thing that people believe in. For instance, you cannot see the wind with your eyes, but when you see autumn leaves being swept through the air and hear the rustling of a summer's breeze as it passes through the trees, you know that it is the wind at work. The wind is invisible, but you have felt its gentle touch on your skin, its fury in a storm, and its cold fingers in an icy gust of wind. We all agree that this is what we call "the wind." But we cannot capture it, put it in a box, and take it out later to show to someone.

Love is like the wind. No one doubts its existence, and we feel it and sense it all around us, but we cannot hold it as we do physical objects. You will never be able to offer tangible proof of love's existence, but everyone can feel its effects. Although we cannot grab hold of love, point to it, and say, "This is love," everyone can feel love when it is present.

How similar love is to God!* Countless people through-

---

* Here, when I say "God," I'm referring to Hermes, who is a part of the soul of El Cantare, therefore, when I use the term "God," in this chapter I'm referring to Lord El Cantare.

out the ages have believed in God and spoken or written about Him, but no one has ever been able to demonstrate proof of God's presence. Throughout history, many sages in many realms of knowledge—people of religion, philosophers, poets, and writers—have grappled with the question of God's existence, but even the greatest among them couldn't produce a shred of tangible evidence to support His existence. Even Jesus Christ could not do so; even he could not point to God, his Heavenly Father, sitting in Heaven, and say to his followers, "Look there. That is God."

Jesus frequently told his followers: "Whoever has seen me has seen the Father... The words that I say to you I do not speak on my own; but the Father who dwells in me does his works" (John 14:9-11). Jesus told people to find God in his words and actions—and they did. Jesus attracted such a large following because people saw God in his powerful sermons and his dignified presence.

This is the way it has been throughout history—the most important things are always the hardest to prove. God, love, courage, wisdom, goodness, kindness, beauty, harmony, progress, mercy, compassion, Truth, sincerity, selflessness: all these exist in abundance in the universe and are known by all beings inhabiting the heavenly worlds. But here in the third dimension, not a single person can conclusively prove their existence. Why? Because they spring from a source that lies outside this material world, in the fourth dimension and beyond. They cannot be proven with the materials of the third dimension.

The great being whom I call the Primordial Buddha, or the Primordial God, inhabits an extremely high dimension that lies beyond the twentieth. Therefore, it is entirely impossible to prove His existence using the instruments and concepts of the three-dimensional world. This is exactly why faith exists. To have faith in something means "to believe" and "to revere or to worship." When we believe in something intangible, we sense its existence and accept it wholeheartedly; when we worship something, we feel humbled by an existence far beyond our own, and pay homage to it.

Jesus Christ said that God is love.* Love is undoubtedly a divine quality of God, but Jesus meant something more. Two millennia ago, Jesus spoke the following words in the land of Nazareth: "God's existence is not meant to be proven. However, if you insist that I describe God to you, I will tell you that God is like love. Love has never proved its existence to anyone. Yet everyone knows how wonderful love is, and everyone seeks to attain it. All people stand witness to its splendor and its power.

"It is the same with faith. Those who believe in the existence of love shall believe in the existence of God. Those

---

*Jesus's statement "God is love" shows that he had reached a level of enlightenment that enabled him to understand that love is Lord El Cantare's most essential nature.

who believe in the power of love shall believe in the power of God, because God *is* love. Behold the works of love that I, Jesus Christ, the son of God, enact. It is not I performing these deeds, but my Father in Heaven, my Lord God, who performs these deeds through me. If you seek to witness love, then behold the deeds I perform. There you will find love, and there you will find God." I know these words because it was I who guided Jesus Christ from Heaven as he spoke them.

3. The Power of Love

Love has no enemies that can stand for long in its path. Love is the greatest force on Earth and in the multidimensional spirit world. In fact, the higher the dimension, the stronger the power of love becomes. This is because love is a force that brings things together. Forces that repel only weaken each other, but forces that unite multiply their individual power.

Love is like an armored all-terrain chariot, an armored vehicle that races through hills and valleys and speeds through rivers and swamps. Love surges onward and braves all evils and anything that tries to block its passage.

Love is light. Love is the lantern that glows in the darkness. Love illuminates the past, the present, and the future.

Love shines in Heaven, on Earth, and into our hearts. Love is the light that dissolves evil with infinite kindness, and engulfs sorrow with unceasing comforting warmth.

Love is life. Love feeds us and nourishes us; it is the source of our strength, the flame of hope, the springboard of our very existence, because love is everything. Without love, there can be no life or death. Without love, we have no passage through life; love is the daily bread of living.

Love is passion. Passion is the power of youth. It is belief in boundless possibilities. Within this passionate energy, we find truth, and we find our life force—our vitality.

Love is courage. Without love, we cannot triumph over evil. Without love, we cannot face death with courage. Love is the torch that lights the fuse of Truth; it is the arrow that pierces the delusions of this world.

Love is a vow. In its name, we promise to live together, speak to one another, and walk beside one another. If love did not exist to unite people, we would journey aimlessly and alone, waiting only for life to come to an end.

Love is words. Without words, love cannot exist; without love, there are no words. Love is manifested through benevolent words, thoughts, vibrations of the mind, and symphonies of the soul. God shapes the world with His words, and through words, His love creates men and women.

Love is harmony. Only through love can people cherish one another, forgive one another, nurture one another, and create a wondrous world together. In the circle of love, there is no anger, no envy, and no jealousy; there is only harmony.

Love is joy. Without love, we cannot know true happiness. Love is the magic that banishes all sorrows from this world, the balm that soothes all wounds. Love brings forth joy, which brings forth more love, circulating in an everlasting cycle. Love is God's way of expressing His boundless delight.

Love is progress. One act of love moves us forward. One loving deed creates light. When our days are filled with love, we take many steps forward, for where there is love, there is no falling back and no fear. Where there is love, there is God. Where there is love, there are countless divine beings. In love, there is only progress; in love, there is only improvement, for love is an act that surges us forward toward God's arms.

Love is eternal. Love is proof that we dwell in eternity. Love existed in the past, exists in the present, and will exist in the future. There has never been a single moment when love did not spread its golden wings and soar through time. Never in history has love vanished completely from our world, for there was always *someone* who loved. Love is the Pegasus that gallops far above the heavenly skies. Love is the hunter who captures the eternal moment of *now*.

Finally, love is prayer. Love cannot exist without prayer, and prayer cannot be offered without love. Prayer has the power to elevate love, to transmute it into something even more potent. Prayer is the secret to making love ever deeper. By praying to God, our wishes for love and about love are fulfilled; in the very act of praying to God, our love is actualized. Prayer increases the positive, active power of love. Through prayer, love can achieve all things.

God is love and love is God. Prayer infuses love with the power of God and strengthens it to its fullest. Through our daily prayer, we live each day, and through prayer, we come to know the face of God. It is through prayer that men and women can exercise love to its fullest.

4. The Mystery of Love

Love is a true mystery. Love's depth and height are infinite, making it impossible to measure. The more we think about love, the deeper and the more fulfilling it becomes. Instead of revealing Himself to us, God sent love to Earth on His behalf. God has given us love as a way to learn about His true nature; we are blessed with the ability to practice and learn from love. Through love, we can sense the presence and power of the invisible and numinous. This is why love is so mystical.

Once upon a time, an old man without children or grandchildren lived in a small shrine on the outskirts of a village. Local urchins often came to play on the shrine, and the most mischievous was Taro, a boy of thirteen who had lost both his parents at an early age and was being raised by his sister.

One day, Taro was playing on the steps of the shrine when three sparrows settled right next to him and started to speak.

"The sun is the greatest thing in this world," the first sparrow said. "Thanks to the sun, we can enjoy the trees, flowers, and an abundant harvest. If the sun were ever to disappear, the world would be dark and colorless. We sparrows always give thanks to the sun, for no creature could survive without it. But humans take it for granted. Filled with a distorted sense of their own importance, they quarrel and even war with each other under the life-giving rays of the sun. I wouldn't be surprised if some day the sun becomes so disappointed that it hides itself forever."

Hearing this, the second sparrow started to speak.

"In my opinion, water is the greatest thing in this world. Nothing can live without it. Without water, the trees and flowers would wither and die within a week, and there certainly wouldn't be any more harvests. Animals like us wouldn't survive even a week. Water is the very source of life and the most wonderful thing in the world. We sparrows are grateful for water, but humans, in their vanity, take it for granted because they believe it is provided for free. They work hard to earn money to buy jewels and ornaments, which aren't useful at all. We sparrows thank God for what He gave us at birth, but humans only strive to become more beautiful, wealthy, and powerful."

Finally, the last sparrow opened its beak.

"The sun and water are certainly marvelous gifts. And you're both right, it seems that humans take for granted the most precious things in this world. But, although no one usually gives it much thought, I think the most important thing in the world is the air we breathe. If the sun were to disappear and the water to dry up, we would still be able to live for a few days. But without air, we would all die in minutes. We sparrows are grateful for the air we fly in, but I've never seen any human give thanks for it. Other creatures, like the mighty whale, give thanks to the air when they come to the surface to fill their lungs. Humans believe that they can fly, but they forget, in their vanity, that airplanes cannot fly without air. The air does so much for us, but it never asks us sparrows or humans for a single penny in return."

After overhearing this conversation, Taro fell deep into thought. He had been taught that humankind was the pinnacle of evolution, but no one he knew had ever spoken with as much wisdom as the sparrows. They were right: he had never thanked the sun, the water, or the air. He thought, "How foolish and ignorant we humans are! We are much less noble than sparrows!"

He jumped to his feet and ran up the steps of the shrine. Finding the old man who lived there, Taro told him what he had just heard. Then Taro burst into tears, saying that he wished he had been born a sparrow. The old man gently replied, "Taro, my boy, you have awakened to an important truth. We humans are fools for having lost sight of what is most important in life, but we know that God forgives us our foolishness because He has bestowed on us the ability to love and care for each other.

"Yes, we humans are fools, but we can't make our foolishness disappear by only paying attention to our mistakes. God gave humans the magic of love, which has the mysterious power to erase our sins and follies. It is because we have this mystical power of love within us that God forgives us and allows us to be the lords of all Creation."

5. Love Has No Enemies

Love is the greatest power that we have. Ultimately, love can never be defeated, and nothing can ever defy its power.

In the course of our lives, we face many trials and setbacks. We actually planned these trials and setbacks ourselves, before our birth, to provide ourselves with opportunities for spiritual growth. For instance, you may have made plans to experience illness, poverty, a broken heart, business failure, conflicts with friends, separations from people you love, or encounters with people you find disagreeable. In addition, we all grow old, our beauty fades, and our bodies become weaker, until finally our time comes to move on to the next world.

If we think of these phenomena as nothing but a random cluster of events, our lives will feel like an endless expanse of hardship and sorrow. But the truth is that adversity is not without meaning, nor is sadness without purpose, because difficult events challenge us to make important choices. They give us chances to choose between a life of giving and a life of taking.

This leads us back to the subject of love. The essence of love is giving. Love is an act of giving; to love is to share with others all of God's blessings, and not to keep them to ourselves. No matter how much we give to others, we need not fear that our well of love will ever run dry, because God is constantly supplying love to us from His infinite store.

The essence of love lies in giving—this is a vitally important point. I know that some of you are suffering because of love. If you are, please ask yourself why you are in agony; why do you hurt from sharing love with others? Because whether or not you are aware of it, *you are seeking something in return for the love you are giving,* and love based on the expectation of repayment is not real. Real love means giving without conditions. The love that you're sharing with others does not actually belong to you in the first place. The love within us that we give comes from God. And because we receive so much love from God, it is only natural that we should repay Him—return our love to Him—by sharing it with others.

Your suffering, then, is caused by feeling that you are giving love but are not being loved in return. This feeling is mistaken. It is not true that people do not love you; it's just that you don't feel loved as much as you had hoped. This is the cause of your distress. At painful times like this, you must remember that the reward for the love you give comes not from those people, but from God Himself.

What does God give us in return? Our reward for loving is that we grow closer to God. The more love we provide others, the closer we become to God. Think about the essence of God. God is like the radiant sun, pouring an abundance of life-giving light upon the Earth without asking for anything in return. Like the sun, God never stops bestowing an endless amount of His love and mercy upon all living creatures. He has never even asked for repayment for giving us life.

So join me on this journey of giving love unconditionally. Take the first step of giving. To give means to think, every single day, about what you can do to make people happy. To give means to pour love onto the hearts of as many people as possible, especially those who are lost in life. It means helping people face setbacks and adversity so they can lead their lives with wisdom and courage.

When you give love, give with wisdom. Giving is not just about giving material things or spoiling others with excessive gifts. True giving requires true nurturing, and to truly nurture others requires wisdom. That is why it is imperative that we have wisdom and courage—so that we can live a life of unconditional giving.

Love is invincible. Nothing can stand in the way of love's path for long. True love is love that gives. True love flows infinitely. True love never expects return. Love is a mighty river that flows from an endless towering height in a spectacular waterfall to land immeasurably far below. Love is the power that gives everything that is ever needed, and its current envelops everything in its path. That is why nothing and no one, including the greatest evil, can stand against the force of this great river.

6. The Stages of Love

Now that we know that real love gives unconditionally, never expecting a reward, we need to learn more about the various stages of love's development, which are not widely understood.

The first stage is *fundamental love*, which is a basic form of "love that gives." This is the love between family members or friends, a type of love with which we are all very familiar. It is the love of a parent for a child, a child for his or her parents, a man for a woman, a woman for a man, one friend or neighbor for another. In its broadest form, fundamental love includes the love we have for the community and the society as a whole.

Fundamental love is something that people feel naturally, which is why it is the basis of all stages of love. We were all born with the ability to give fundamental love, and we intrinsically know how wonderful this form of love is; we inherently experience happiness through acts of giving love. Yet, though we might understand this fundamental and most common form of love, putting it into practice is a different matter and can sometimes be difficult, as we know from our own experiences.

Despite the challenges involved, if everyone could at least practice this first level of love, our world would be transformed into Heaven. Literally. It would shift from the third dimension—this physical world on Earth—into the fifth dimension in the spirit world, the World of Goodness. That is why practicing fundamental love is the first step to creating Heaven on Earth.

The second level in the development of love is *spiritually nurturing love*. Although fundamental love is not easy to put into practice consistently, everyone has an innate potential to exercise it. This is not the case with spiritually nurturing love, however. In fact, not everyone has the ability to put spiritually nurturing love into practice because it is a love that leads—a love that flows from a great height and travels downstream. Those who provide this second form of love are capable people who, through great efforts, have developed their abilities enough to be leaders who show people the way; they have attained a level of excellence that inspires others to turn to them for leadership.

Spiritually nurturing love is an intellectual and rational type of love. You cannot truly lead others until you have developed the intellect and the insight to grasp the actual conditions of current society. Leaders must possess acute powers of reasoning so that they can solve the problems they find. To become true leaders, we must exercise firmness and even sternness, at times, for we must be able to warn those in danger of spiritual regression that they need to turn back toward the right path. Since the blind cannot lead the blind, we must build character by attaining excellence so that we can practice this love. Spiritually nurturing love is the love practiced in the World of Light, the sixth dimension of Heaven, so those leaders on Earth who are capable of practicing this love are already attuned to this part of Heaven.

So far, we have looked at fundamental love, which springs from natural inclination, and spiritually nurturing love, the love that leads, which is born of excellence and leadership. These are wonderful forms of love, but there is a kind of love that transcends them both, a love that goes beyond talents, knowledge, and worldly efforts. This is the third level of love: *forgiving love.*

People who practice forgiving love have already been through a transformative spiritual awakening; many virtuous leaders in religion have possessed forgiving love. It is a love that transcends the dichotomy of good and evil and is a state of mind completely devoted to one's sacred mission. Those at this level know that all who live in the material world are spiritually blind, groping through the darkness without a light to show them the path or a hand to guide them. To realize this fact, you must have awakened to the truth of your own foolishness and felt deep remorse for it. Only those who have found the light within their own suffering can identify the blinders that cover people's eyes and still love the divine nature within them. This state of mind, of forgiving love, arrives only after we have attained a virtue that surpasses skill: a magnanimous and merciful heart.

All people are God's children, and therefore, all people have a part of God in them. Only people who perceive this truth can recognize the divine nature of even their enemies and foes. Buddhism calls this state of mind *transcendental wisdom.* Those who can exercise forgiving love are envoys of the seventh dimension; they are attuned to the World of Bodhisattvas. The state of forgiving is the state of the bodhisattva.

It is important, however, that forgiving love not be mistakenly used to encourage devils who try to hinder God's love from reaching people—devils whose very existence is the antithesis of love. Bodhisattvas fight against these devils using faith and selfless wrath as weapons. Indeed, some devils enter the gates of forgiveness for the first time when they realize that they can never win against Buddha or God. For this reason, it is sometimes necessary to practice an active form of forgiving love, one that fights evil and leads to redemption.

7. Love Incarnate and God's Love

I would now like to share with you an even higher state of love. What form of love could be higher than forgiving love? I call it *love incarnate*. This love goes beyond the love of one person for another, and it goes beyond the status-related love that is associated with leadership and forgiveness.

Love incarnate occurs when a person's very being emanates love. Even the briefest encounter with love incarnate will free you from worries and suffering, awaken you to the Truths, guide you to feel remorse for your mistakes, and return you to the right path. People who are love incarnate light up the world, bringing the flame of hope to all humankind. Their love is not necessarily expressed to a particular person, or by the beautiful words they speak, or through the kindness they show. They *are* love, and whenever they are present, love itself is present. They are love personified.

People who embody love have been present throughout the history of humankind, their gifts a beacon to the ages. Love incarnate is associated with the giants of history, those who have towered above the rest by serving as the light of the world and becoming the very spirit of their age. Theirs is a love that radiates out in all directions, passing from themselves to countless masses and making them the embodiment of light.

As you have probably guessed, this love belongs to the World of Tathagatas of the eighth dimension. Someone who embodies love in a particular historical period is actually the incarnation of a tathagata; the very fact that this person has been born on Earth is a great blessing for all humankind because their compassion is a light that shines impartially on all people. It is not a relative love, which varies in strength depending on the person to whom it is being given: a tathagata's compassion is absolute and unbiased.

As we've seen, the various levels of love correlate to specific spiritual dimensions. Fundamental love corresponds to the fifth dimension; spiritually nurturing love corresponds to the sixth; forgiving love corresponds to the seventh dimension; and love incarnate corresponds to the eighth. It is especially valuable to see this correlation as our spiritual training brings us to higher levels of love. (I have purposely not mentioned a form of love that corresponds to the fourth dimension, which is called *instinctive love*. Depending on how you direct this love, it can attune either to Hell or to the Astral Realm in Heaven, so this is not a love that we should aim for in our spiritual discipline.)

The highest form of love for the people of planet Earth is that of the ninth dimension. This love is known as *an embodiment of God's love*, and *the love of a Savior*. However, this is too high a form of love for the majority of people to even aspire to. This is the level of love practiced by Grand Spirits such as Shakyamuni Buddha and Jesus Christ—those who have received the divine command of God, whom we also call Buddha, to become His instruments and His greatest envoys. Most of us must be content with simply knowing that there is a level above love incarnate—God's love—that expresses His fathomless compassion for all humankind by guiding our ongoing evolution. This love is also known as Buddha's compassion.

The act of distorting the words of God or Buddha, of conveying them incorrectly, is the gravest crime of all, more harmful than robbery or even murder. If religious leaders or other people falsely proclaim themselves to be saviors, what awaits them after death is not the heights of the ninth dimension but the deepest pits of the fourth dimension's Abysmal Hell. How could this be a graver crime than murder? Because it harms the eternal soul, which is far more precious than any single incarnate lifetime spent on Earth.

To sum things up, the developmental stages of love are as follows: the instinctive love of the fourth dimension, which does not require any effort and is not a goal to which we aspire; fundamental love; spiritually nurturing love; forgiving love; love incarnate; and finally, God's love, which is beyond the scope of human endeavor.

8. Love and the Eightfold Path

In chapter 2, I described "Buddha's Teaching: The Eightfold Path," and in this chapter, I have explored the various levels of love. Now I would like to explain the relationship between these two teachings.

As we've seen, following the Eightfold Path allows us to live righteously as human beings, making daily discoveries that lead us toward enlightenment. We've also seen that love has four levels to which we can aspire: fundamental love, spiritually nurturing love, forgiving love, and love incarnate. The Eightfold Path focuses on the spiritual discipline we undergo and the enlightenment we achieve on a *daily basis*, while the stages of love help us bring *longer-term* goals to our daily spiritual practice.

If we make a close comparison between the Eightfold

Path and the stages of love, we reach the following conclusions:

> Right View and Right Speech
>> correspond to fundamental love;
> Right Action and Right Livelihood
>> correspond to spiritually nurturing love;
> Right Thought and Right Effort
>> correspond to forgiving love;
> Right Mindfulness and Right Concentration
>> correspond to love incarnate.

Let me explain this a bit more fully. First, how do Right View and Right Speech correspond to fundamental love? Fundamental love is love for a person that you would naturally tend to care about. To practice this love properly, we need to have a good understanding of that person, to see that person as they truly are. To be able to hold proper perceptions of others, our perceptions need a foundation of right faith so that we can distinguish right from wrong and good from bad. In practicing this form of love, we also need to be able to discern what problems the people we love might be facing and what help they might need, without being blinded by preconceptions. This is the practice of Right View. To express fundamental love, we must also practice Right Speech, offering words of advice that will be helpful and not harmful. We need to find the right words that will wrap the hearts of others in the warmth of love and help them overcome their difficulties.

Next, we look at how Right Action and Right Livelihood correspond to spiritually nurturing love. During Shakyamuni Buddha's life, Right Action meant observing Buddhist principles, such as not killing any living creatures or committing any sins of the flesh. Translated into today's terms, Right Action means not resorting to violence, not stealing, being faithful to your spouse, being a person of strong morals and ethical values, respecting other people's rights, and serving as a role model.

Right Livelihood is the practice of living a spiritually righteous and fulfilling life. To practice Right Livelihood is to avoid any occupation or ways of earning a living that would oppose Buddha's Truths, and to refrain from addictive or destructive behaviors such as joining gangs, becoming involved with organized crime, or making money in the sex industry. We should also live upright and healthy lifestyles: we must avoid excessive alcohol; addiction to all forms of gambling, as well as cigarettes, drugs, and other substances; and incurring unnecessary debt. Right Livelihood ultimately comes down to striving for a spiritual and religious way of life, because living with faith creates an environment that fosters spiritually nurturing love. We humans cannot live alone, and we pass every day of our lives in the company of others. All of us live in communities, and it is part of being human to support others and offer guidance when it is needed. Therefore, the more that people practice Right Livelihood and aspire to create Utopia in their homes, the closer we come to actualizing Heaven on Earth. In these ways, Right Action and Right Livelihood correspond to and support the state of spiritually nurturing love.

Third, Right Thought and Right Effort support the state of forgiving love. Right Thought involves not giving in to greed, anger, or ignorance (Buddhism's Three Poisons of the Mind), nor to conceit, doubt, or false views (which, taken together with the Three Poisons of the Mind, make up Buddhism's Six Primary Afflictions). These states of mind cloud our judgment.[5] Right Thought is the practice of studying our relationships through the eyes of the Truths, and thinking about where any adjustment or improvement might be required. We must not allow ourselves to be deluded by what we see with our physical eyes. Instead, we should imagine how the people we interact with might appear in the spirit world, and form our relationships based on that understanding. If as we reflect deeply into the recesses of our minds, we discover any wrong-minded views or thoughts, we should feel genuine remorse and correct them. Then we should think about *how each of us should be* as children of Buddha. That contemplation should give you a picture of everyone pursuing great harmony as we guide and support each other. Ultimately, the more you think with Right Thoughts, the more magnanimity and acceptance will fill your heart and mind, bringing you naturally toward the state of forgiving love.

Right Effort, the study and practice of the Truths, also leads to the state of forgiving love. When we practice Right Effort, we take the path of avoiding temptations and pursuing and learning Buddha's Truths; we strive to fill our minds with good and righteous ideals and thoughts. Through this journey toward Him, your enlightenment will grow every day, and the power of your virtue will gradually multiply in strength. You will no longer find anger, constant dissatisfactions, grumbling, or jealousy arising in your mind. Your daily life will become so filled with virtuous right thoughts that it will align itself with the project of creating peace on Earth. Your mind will become unshakable, and you will acquire the power to help purify the sins of those who have erred. The better you become at practicing Right Effort, the deeper your religious and spiritual awareness and discernment will become, and the closer you will draw to the state of forgiving love.

Fourth, Right Mindfulness and Right Concentration correspond to and support love incarnate. Right Mindfulness is the practice of focusing your mind on living in accord with Buddha's Truths. It involves envisioning your future with a calm mind, forming plans accordingly, and praying that you will achieve righteous self-realization as His children. This righteous self-realization is a perfected state of being a human child of Buddha, and a state of becoming one with Him—the state of a tathagata. It is the loftiest state any human being can achieve; the very presence of a tathagata shines light onto the world and draws the world's respect. Right Mindfulness is aimed at achieving this, the highest goal of a righteous life.

Right Concentration refers to the ultimate state for seekers of Buddha's Truths and people of faith. Since ancient times, spiritual seekers have practiced different methods of meditation—such as yoga, Zen, contemplation, and reflective meditation—in an effort to achieve enlightenment and communicate with Divine Spirits. There are three levels of Right Concentration. At the first level, you practice self-reflection every day and become capable of communicating with your guardian spirit. When you reach the next level, you can communicate with Guiding Spirits who help you carry out your specific mission in this life. At the third and final level, you can contact the Great Guiding Spirits of Light, the inhabitants of the World of Tathagatas in the eighth dimension.

How is this possible? There is a spiritual teaching that the mind can attune to three thousand worlds: the mind of a human being can be attuned to countless different areas of the spirit world. This means that if you could achieve the enlightenment of a tathagata in your right meditation, you would be able to communicate with the Great Guiding Spirits of the eighth dimension. All tathagatas in physical bodies on Earth are receiving spiritual guidance, either directly or indirectly, from Great Guiding Spirits of upper levels. At the very least, they are certainly receiving inspirations from Heaven that are helping them fulfill their mission on Earth. To reach the state of love incarnate, we must practice Right Concentration, which helps us achieve spiritual emancipation and become capable of concentrating our minds perfectly.

Now we know that just as we practice love in stages, we should also practice the Eightfold Path in stages. These stages can be arranged into four levels: Right View and Right Speech → Right Action and Right Livelihood → Right Thought and Right Effort → Right Mindfulness and Right Concentration. (This order is different from that of Shakyamuni Buddha's, but it is particularly effective for beginners.*) These four stages are in keeping with the four levels of love: fundamental love, spiritually nurturing love, forgiving love, and love incarnate. You must master one stage of the Eightfold Path to move on to the next, and the same is true of love. But in both cases, it is most important to master the first stage.

---

* Happy Science members, who should be eagerly undertaking spiritual training, should put into practice the teachings found in the prayer "Words of Emancipation: Buddha's Teaching, The Eightfold Path," from our basic sutra, *Buddha's Teaching: The Dharma of the Right Mind.*

9. *The Love of Angels*

Now let's turn our attention from people who receive love and put it into practice to the angels in Heaven who provide this love. In general, those spirits whom most people know as *angels* inhabit the highest realm of the sixth dimension and the higher dimensions above the sixth dimension. This group of spirits includes the guardian deities of upper sixth dimension, bodhisattvas in the seventh dimension, tathagatas in the eighth dimension, and Grand Tathagatas in the ninth dimension, where they are also known as gurus or advanced Great Guiding Spirits of Light.

The way these elevated spirits express their love varies. Arhats of the sixth dimension, also known as angels of light, manifest their love in three ways: as the love of guardian deities directed at people on Earth; as the love given to souls in Hell toward their salvation; and as the love of those who educate the souls that inhabit the World of Goodness in the fifth dimension.

Bodhisattvas of light, also known as angels, of the seventh dimension express their love in four ways. The first is by being born on Earth and becoming a leader in any specific field, including religion. The second is by serving as assistants to the Great Guiding Spirits, the tathagatas of higher dimensions. The third way that bodhisattvas express their love is by being in charge of guiding souls in Hell to salvation. The fourth is by supplying Buddha's light to the spirit worlds of the sixth dimension and below.

In the eighth dimension, tathagatas of light, also known as archangels, express their love in five ways. The first is the love expressed by great religious leaders, who are born on Earth every few hundred years to found new religions or start religious reforms that create new teachings. The second is by teaching bodhisattvas; every bodhisattva has a tathagata for a teacher, and one tathagata teaches many bodhisattvas. The third is by serving as high commanders of teams that fight Satan in Hell and try to convert him. The fourth is spreading one of the seven colors of Buddha's light—for example, the light of love. The fifth expression is a very creative kind of love: administering the design of new civilizations.

The love of Grand Tathagatas of light of the ninth dimension encompasses all forms of love, but it can be roughly divided into the following six variations. The first is the love of a savior who appears on Earth every few thousand years to found a religion that will purify the world. The second is the love of a grand teacher who gives guidance from Heaven to saviors on Earth. The third advances the progress and evolution of humankind. The fourth is a love that serves as the source of one of the seven colors of Buddha's light that shine on the worlds of the eighth dimension and below. The fifth is the love of the regulator who preserves distinctions and order in the spirit world. This form of love regulates and manages the standards by which all souls' states of mind are evaluated. Finally, the sixth expression of love is to take responsibility for Earth's plans as a planet, within the vast plans of the universe.

10. *The Great River of Love*

In this chapter, I have discussed many aspects of human love, as well as the love of various types of angels. Together, we have come to the realization that there must be a love that flows through this world of the third dimension and beyond to the multidimensional spirit world. This love is the river of life, a never-ending source of vitality. If you could perceive it as I do, with spiritual sight, it would appear as a tremendous flood of energy, one vast river flowing from infinite heights. You would see this river of love become a spectacular water-fall, cascading from the ninth dimension to the third.

If you could see this astounding view of the river of love, you would know that nothing in this world could ever stand in defiance of its unceasing and overwhelming force. Nothing can oppose love's mighty force of vitality; for this reason, in the end, love has no enemies. Do you imagine that Hell is powerful enough to fight against Heaven, the kingdom of God, also known as Buddha? Do you think of Hell as an enormous place with a force equal to that of Heaven? If you do, you are gravely mistaken. The mighty currents of God's river of love, which is also known as Buddha's river of love, engulf everything in its path. Hell is just a small world located in a corner of the fourth dimension, the salt water at the mouth of the river of God's love. It can try to mix its materialism, worldly desires, delusion, and evil into the fresh water that flows by, but the fresh water of Heaven easily sweeps them aside. Hell is like a tiny ailing tumor that has appeared within the great world of God, also known as Buddha.

Love is light. Just as darkness cannot withstand light, evil cannot successfully defy love. Hell cannot block the river of love. From ancient times, people have imagined Hell as a world equal in size to Heaven, where angels and demons fight pitched battles with each other. But this is not the way it is. People on Earth overestimate the influence of Hell only because Hell is located very near the third dimension and its spiritual vibrations are close at hand. Heaven stretches from the Posthumous World of the fourth dimension all the way up to the highest dimensions, whereas Hell is only a muddy lake within the fourth dimension where the light does not reach. It is true that this muddy lake is large enough to sustain a population of several billion. However, just as water evaporates beneath the rays of the sun, Hell is destined to vanish.

What, in fact, are the elements of Hell? The energies whirling around the atmosphere of Hell are envy; jealousy; reactive rage; grumbling; excessive desire; dissatisfaction; pessimism; negativism; indecisiveness; cowardice; laziness; self-hatred; grudges; hatred; cursing; lust; aggression; egotism; abusive speech; deceit; manic depression; drunken frenzy; violence; exclusionism; lies;

falsehood; materialism; atheism; alienation; authoritarianism; greed for money, status, and fame; and disharmony. These are all forms of negative energy, but in truth, they do not really exist as entities unto themselves. Hatred, jealousy, rage, and dissatisfaction, for instance, are just the results of an absence of love. Hell itself is simply the product of a lack of love.

In the final analysis, the spirits in Hell are not powerful beings who can effectively oppose the light of Heaven; they are just souls longing to be loved. Deep inside, they crave kindness. They are unfortunate beings in distress, in need of someone to rescue them from their suffering. In truth, they are sick hospital patients suffering from "love deficiency syndrome." Real love is based on giving, but spirits in Hell endlessly crave care and attention. The inhabitants of Hell were once residents of Earth who never came to understand the nature of love, so they kept taking and taking love from others until they died. As a result, they are now suffering in Hell.

It is not too late to make Hell disappear once and for all. How can we accomplish this? The answer lies in creating awareness among all people that the essence of love is *giving*, and in basing our lives on this knowledge. And we can begin to give by expressing gratitude. When we give thanks to Buddha for providing us with all we need, a sacred desire arises within us to repay Him for the world He created. This is the moment when we begin a lifetime on the path of love; this is our first step toward giving with no thought of return.

THE ULTIMATE
ENLIGHTENMENT

1. What Is Enlightenment?

Throughout the ages, human beings have always sought enlightenment. Some of us may not know exactly what enlightenment is, but we all have an undeniable desire to develop our
souls. It's woven into the very fabric of our humanity. Enlightenment is generally associated with religion, but it also
holds a central place in the field of philosophy, which reflects
both our philosophical desire to pursue the Truths and our
yearning for an intellectual understanding of the mysteries
and workings of the world. Whether or not Confucianism
is a religion is open to discussion, but there's no doubt that
Confucius also tried to enlighten people by teaching them
his particular path to the state of moral perfection.

In this chapter, I would like to focus on religious enlightenment, which encompasses a philosophical desire to attain the Truths and pursue human perfection. The heart of religious enlightenment is our connection to Buddha. We strengthen that connection and grow closer to Him by exploring the principles of the world that He created. In this respect, there is no end to the path of enlightenment. To put it another way, we can never attain complete enlightenment, no matter how much effort we put forth. It's almost impossible to gain a complete understanding of the entire spirit world or to attain the ultimate state. Fortunately, however, there are different levels of enlightenment. In other words, it's possible for all people to attain a certain level of enlightenment, in keeping with their own spiritual awareness. There is also an ultimate level of enlightenment for human beings dwelling in physical bodies on Earth. In this chapter, I would like to describe the different stages leading to this highest level of enlightenment attainable for human beings.

Of all the religious leaders and great masters in human history, Shakyamuni Buddha (Gautama Siddhartha), who preached the Laws more than 2,500 years ago in India, pursued the most intensive exploration of enlightenment. From the time he attained great enlightenment under the Bodhi tree and became the Buddha, his level of enlightenment continued to rise until he entered Nirvana at the age of eighty under the sal trees outside Kushinagar Palace. While Shakyamuni's life story appears in many popular books and scholarly publications, most of these texts capture only fragments of his philosophy and fail to convey the state of ultimate enlightenment that he was able to attain.

Within the mind exists a wondrous world. I opened the window of my mind several decades ago and began communing with my subconscious in the spirit world. Since then, I have been able to gain access to the memories of past spiritual masters and to directly experience how they felt, what they thought, what they did, and what part of the Truths they grasped. I know exactly what Shakyamuni Buddha was thinking as he meditated under the Bodhi tree and attained enlightenment. Although it happened more than 2,500 years ago, I can feel it as if it were happening this very moment.

This chapter will provide a new perspective on enlightenment in today's world, while focusing on the enlightenment of Shakyamuni Buddha. My goal is to pass on to future generations the wisdom that will help them achieve enlightenment. This method to attain enlightenment is both our legacy from the past and our hope for the future.

2. The Benefits of Enlightenment

What is the purpose of humankind's search for enlightenment? What could be gained from attaining an enlightened state? To answer these questions, we must first consider our true purpose and mission in life, beginning with the reason human beings are born into this world to dwell in physical bodies.

Before you were born, you were a spirit in Heaven with the freedom to live as you pleased. In Heaven, you don't need food or drink. You don't have to earn a living. You don't need to spend nine months in a mother's womb, or weep with hunger and frustration as an infant and child. You don't have to fight with your parents or be distressed by the sexual issues of adolescence. You don't have to struggle financially or have the disheartening experience of working for someone you don't like or respect. You don't have to suffer from separation from your loved ones, or from illness, or from the indignities, aches, and pains of growing old. You don't have to experience being abandoned by your children or grandchildren. You don't have to go through the grief of losing your spouse or the fear of your own death. In Heaven, you don't have to endure any of the suffering that is inescapable here on Earth.

Heaven is a world where we can see into one another's minds as if they were the clearest glass. Those whose thoughts do not promote harmony cannot stay in that world, which means that in Heaven, you only meet people who deeply understand and care for you, and about whom you feel the same way. Heaven is a Utopia where every resident has achieved at least a basic level of enlightenment: they realize that they should love and help each other.

Spirits in Heaven can change their age and appearance as they like. When they focus their will on manifesting something, it appears. Everyone in Heaven strives to improve their soul by deepening their understanding of the Truths. By contrast, spirits in Hell are full of discordant and destructive thoughts. Because of this, these spirits cannot reincarnate on Earth directly from Hell.

What do they need to do to reincarnate on Earth? First they need to return to Heaven, where they must meet the minimum requirements for entering the Astral Realm in the fourth dimension. To put this another way, these spirits cannot be born on Earth again unless they understand, to a greater or lesser extent, that they are spiritual beings and children of Buddha. To earn this spiritual awakening, they must reflect on their thoughts and deeds and realize where they went wrong. For those who have spent many years in Hell and have finally completed their self-reflection, returning to Heaven is the first step in a process that can lead to a new reincarnation—a chance to start over as human beings in this world.

For those in Heaven, reincarnation on Earth is always a trial—literally—because our world has been designated as a training ground for souls. By being born into physical bodies, souls in Heaven test the authenticity of their spiritual awakening to their divine nature. It's easy for souls in Heaven to believe in Buddha when they have spiritual freedom. But when they are bound by the rules of this three-dimensional material world, they face real tests: whether or not they can find faith, how much they can understand the workings of the fourth dimension and beyond, and how much of His power they can discover at work in this physical world. Only those who pass these intensive tests can return to a higher world than the one they came here from.

Most souls who have suffered long years in Hell and have finally attained the necessary level of enlightenment to be born into Earth are fiercely determined to lead a worthy life. However, some are strongly affected by the coarse vibrations of the material world and end up indulging deeply in worldly temptations. Since these spirits can't awaken to their true nature as children of Buddha, they will fall into an even deeper chamber of Hell instead of returning to Heaven at a higher level.

Although this three-dimensional physical world provides trials for souls, it also offers them an opportunity that they can't find in Heaven. Because people from different dimensions gather in this world, we on Earth can meet people that we might never encounter in the more hierarchical spirit world. We can see a Great Guiding Spirit of Light in the flesh, for example, or talk to someone whose mind is attuned to Satan in Hell. No matter what dimension they come from, all people stand at the same starting line when they are born into a new life here. When we awaken to the Truth of life, we are given a chance to start our lives over again.

3. Ways to Attain Enlightenment

As we've now seen, enlightenment is a process of developing your spirituality and manifesting your divine nature through the system of reincarnation. When you search for the best way to improve your soul, you find that numerous paths open before you, each with its own method of spiritual training. Different religions, including Buddhism, Christianity, Islam, Confucianism, Shintoism, and Taoism, have their own specific forms of spiritual discipline. Indeed, this is why people in search of the path to Buddha often become lost in the maze of faith. They get caught up in determining which religion is correct, instead of which practice is right for their spiritual training.

All major world religions are in some way or other manifestations of Buddha's light. These religions have inspired people for thousands of years and have gained the respect of countless people. The founders of such religions have been revered for so long because their lives emit the brilliant light of Buddha's energy. Although all religions originate from the same light source, each takes on a unique color because of differences in the time, ethnicity, culture, and even climate of the region in which the teachings were given. In any case, the teachings of the past are past; what we urgently need now are new teachings for the coming age. We must find new ways of training our souls on Earth in the current era.

Ways of attaining enlightenment are, in short, ways of attuning your mind to the mind of Buddha. To seek enlightenment is to explore how you can live with the His Will as your own. It is to search for the way to live in accord with the Truths. One way to do this is to practice the Eightfold Path, and another is to practice the developmental stages of love. If you wish to seek the Buddhist path to enlightenment, I recommend that you practice the Eightfold Path daily and use it as a guide for your life. You will discover universal Truths in the Eightfold Path, and you will find an eternal path to human perfection. The Eightfold Path is a practical method for attaining the state of enlightenment, which you will need more than a lifetime to reach. You will be able to master the essence of the Truths only when you can see, think, speak, act, and live in the right way; make the right effort; have the right will; and practice right meditation. But it will not be easy, and for some it may not even be possible to master the Eightfold Path.

For first-timers, it will probably take at least five to ten years to be able to practice Right View and Right Speech properly. Once you feel confident practicing them, the next step is to concentrate on practicing Right Action and Right Livelihood every day. If you can practice these four paths correctly, you will be able to achieve the level of enlightenment required to enter the World of Light in the sixth dimension. When you start practicing Right Thought and Right Effort, you are entering an authentic religious life. If you can keep an unshakable mind no matter what hardships you face, you have achieved the state of arhat, which is what you need to move up from the World of Light in the sixth dimension to the World of Bodhisattvas of the seventh dimension. Reaching this level means that you have completed basic spiritual training. However, you have not yet achieved the state of arhat if you become upset by people's remarks, fly into a rage over trifling matters, or feel driven by the desire for social status or fame in this world.

Take a good look at the minds and deeds of contemporary religious leaders around the world. Some concentrate only on gaining psychic powers, while others take advantage of others' weaknesses and deceive them. Some even extort money from their followers by threatening them with Hell or other cursed states. Such people have a long way to go before reaching the state of arhat, which is the step before becoming a bodhisattva, or an angel. True religious leaders sent from Heaven are not swayed by lust for power, fame, money, or sex; nor do they fall prey to anger, hatred, or discontent.

4. Tathata

When you attain the state of arhat, you have the strong faith and unshakable mind with which to withstand worldly troubles. You can receive guidance from your guardian spirit on a daily basis, and you can understand the feelings of others as if you are seeing through their minds. In other words, you have become spiritually mature, and as a religious person, you have reached a level where you can teach and guide people.

Nonetheless, even at this stage, you are still in danger of falling down the ladder of enlightenment. You haven't grasped the scale, height, and depth of the teachings of Buddha's Truths, nor have you gained access to the enlightenment of bodhisattvas, which means that you are still at high risk of being misled by disbelief and evil thoughts. If you attune your mind to the spirits that reside in the Tengu Realm and the Sennin Realm in Minor Heaven,* you may be tempted by rudimentary spiritual ability that grants you psychic power and the ability to cause spiritual phenomena. Instead of seeking such supernatural powers, however, you should deepen your love and continue your pursuit of higher levels of enlightenment. And never forget the significance of studying the Truths.

One reason people tumble from the state of arhat is that they neglect their efforts to polish their minds. If your mind

---

* The spirit world is made up of many different realms layered both horizontally and vertically. Minor Heaven exists on the back side of Heaven, and consists of various realms inhabited by spirits who exclusively focus on exercising metaphysical forces. They do not place value on love or enlightenment, and thus tend to lack human warmth and kindness. (Refer to *The Nine Dimensions*. IRH Press, 2012)

were made of metal, you would need to remove all the rust and make it shine to attain the state of arhat. Even so, it would get rusty again if you forgot to polish it. If you do not notice that your mind is getting rusty because you're convinced that you are a great master who has become enlightened, then you are in great danger of falling.

When your mind has been polished to a bright sparkle, its surface is very smooth, which makes it capable of repelling negative energy, no matter how evil such energy may be. But when your mind gets rusty, its surface becomes rough, and all sorts of negative thoughts and ideas stick to it. What's more, devils in Hell can drive pitons into the receptive surface of your mind and hang ropes that reach down into the depths of Hell. Various creatures, including lost souls, animal souls, and even Satan, can climb up the ropes from the world of darkness and creep into your mind. Some religious leaders, in spite of having managed to reach the state of arhat, allow evil to sneak into their minds this way. This evil confuses them, infiltrates their teaching, and leads them to ruin people's lives. This is a most dangerous pitfall.

So never forget how vital it is to keep your mind free of rust at all times. Remove the rust and polish your mind until it shines. If you let devils climb into your mind, you're in deep trouble. As long as you provide access, devils will find the way to creep inside you, no matter how many times you try to exorcise them. You won't be able to achieve true salvation merely through exorcism or an act of spiritual purification; only a polished mind can protect you from invasions from Hell. This is why maintaining a shining mind is crucial. Studying and practicing the Truths can help you remove the rust and keep your mind polished, and such practice of repelling evil is a prerequisite to higher enlightenment.

So the first step to attaining the higher levels of enlightenment is to reach the state of arhat, which is a pure state of mind undisturbed by worldly matters. In this state, you can communicate with your guardian spirit and sense the feelings and thoughts of others as if they were your own. Until you attain this state of mind, you will not be able to pursue further spiritual training or attain a higher level of enlightenment. First, aim to achieve the state of arhat. You will discover the world of true awakening only when you reach an even higher level of enlightenment than that of the sixth dimension.

What is the deeper awareness, the higher enlightenment that transcends the enlightenment of arhat? The state of enlightenment above arhat is known as *tathata*. When you attain tathata, you can receive guidance from spirits at higher levels of Heaven and commune with them spiritually. These Guiding Spirits are from the seventh dimension or above, and usually reside in a higher world than the world of your own guardian spirit. When you reach this state, you are virtually indomitable. Except under the most extreme conditions, you will no longer fall into the hands of devils and demons. Once you start receiving guidance from tathagatas and bodhisattvas, you emit light that fends off all evil.

When you attain the state of tathata, arrogance is no longer possible; you are always humble. Your main concern is finding ways to help and serve others, save those lost in life, and contribute to the world. Conceit is the main reason people fall from the state of arhat, but once you achieve the indomitable state of tathata, you no longer have egotistical or self-centered thoughts and desires. Your mind always remains calm. It is at this stage that you can practice Right Mindfulness and Right Concentration in the truest sense.

In the state of tathata, you also gain a new spiritual ability. Then, as you approach the *next* level of awareness—the state of boundless perception—you attain a complete understanding of other people, even if they are hundreds of miles away. For example, just by bringing someone's name to mind, you can instantly grasp her current state, her worries, and the spirits that are influencing her, as well as gain access to all her past lives and her future incarnations, even if that person is on the opposite side of the globe. This is a remarkable ability, however it's important to keep refining and deepening your love and wisdom and not become completely absorbed in the power of second sight.

5. Boundless Perception

Tathata is the state of bodhisattvas, those who know the secrets of the spirit world. There are different levels of tathata, and its highest level can lead to the World of Tathagatas. But generally, tathata refers to the state of bodhisattvas who reside above arhats. It describes not only people on Earth, but also spirits in Heaven who have attained this level of enlightenment.

As we've seen, spirits in Heaven don't necessarily know everything. The scope of their understanding varies depending on the bandwidth of their perspective and the level of their enlightenment. A good example of this is the ability to foretell the future. All spirits of the fourth dimension and beyond can foretell future events, but their predictions about events on Earth are not necessarily accurate, which can cause trouble.

There are two reasons for these discrepancies. Future events can be divided into two categories: fixed and fluid. Fixed events have been set by the Divine Spirits and cannot be changed, except under extraordinary circumstances. On the other hand, fluid events are only likely to happen if the situation remains the same. Fluid events can be changed through the efforts of people on Earth and by the guidance of guardian spirits and Guiding Spirits. This is one reason that the prophecies of the spirits in Heaven may not come true. The second reason is that the degree of accuracy of spirit predictions varies widely depending on a given spirit's level of spiritual awareness and area of expertise. Generally speaking, the higher the level of spirituality, the more accurate the prophecy. Some spirits specialize in foreseeing future events, so their predictions tend to be more reliable.

Now I would like to move on to describe the state of enlightenment one step higher than that of tathata: the state of *avalokitesvara,* or boundless perception. The Buddhist Heart Sutra starts with a phrase that means, "Avalokitesvara Bodhisattva* has deepened her spiritual awareness and discovered the reservoir of her inner subconscious." Here, Avalokitesvara Bodhisattva does not refer to a particular person, but to the higher state of mind that bodhisattvas can attain through spiritual training. Even when you attain the enlightenment of a bodhisattva and are determined to save the people of the world, you will not be completely free from personal worries and suffering, which often limit the ability to use supernatural powers. But as you advance further in your spiritual training, you will be able to attain a higher level of enlightenment known as the state of *brahma.* You will then be able to exert divine supernatural powers consistently, regardless of personal obstacles such as illness, mishaps, or relationship

---

* Avalokitesvara Bodhisattva is a Sanskrit name and is often translated as Guanshiyin or Kanzeon Bodhisattva ("Lord who perceives the world's lamentations"), or the Goddess of Mercy.

problems. Avalokitesvara Bodhisattvas are souls that have attained the state of brahma and reside in a realm between the World of Bodhisattvas of the seventh dimension and the World of Tathagatas of the eighth dimension.

When you reach this state of mind, you will acquire all six divine supernatural powers to some extent. These supernatural powers are clairvoyance, clairaudience, mind reading, fate reading, astral travel, and spiritual wisdom.* Clairvoyance is second sight, the ability to see people's auras and the spirits that are influencing them. It also lets us see through the spirit world. Clairaudience is the ability to hear voices of spirits in the other world, which makes it possible to receive spiritual messages. Mind reading is the ability to perceive what's in other people's minds and to feel their emotions as if they were our own. Fate reading is the ability to see one's own future and to foretell that of others; it also includes the ability to access the memories of other people's souls and see people's past lives. Astral travel is teleportation to the spirit world, a process in which your soul leaves your physical body. Spiritual wisdom is the power to stop deluded thoughts and transcend all physical desires. Confucius described this state of mind when he pro-

---

* Here, spiritual wisdom refers to the ability to free oneself of all worldly delusions. It is achieved through the daily practice of self-reflection. While the other five powers describe psychic abilities, this sixth power is a form of highly advanced wisdom. Once you attain this spiritual wisdom, it's possible to live an outwardly normal life even if you possess extraordinary psychic powers.

claimed: "I followed my heart's desire without transgressing what is right" (*The Analects of Confucious* 2:4). This ability lets us persist in efforts to refine our minds through diligent spiritual discipline, even after we acquire spiritual powers.

When you attain the state of boundless perception, you have acquired all six of these divine supernatural powers to a certain extent. This is a higher spiritual level than the state of tathata.

6. One Is Many—Many Are One

Now I would like to explore the state of mind you can attain after gaining the deepest understanding of Right Thought, Right Effort, Right Mindfulness, and Right Concentration. This is the level of enlightenment you attain when you reach the stage of love incarnate in the developmental stages of love. Put simply, I would like to describe the enlightenment of tathagatas.

The souls in the World of Bodhisattvas and below generally see themselves and each other as having a human appearance, even though souls are essentially intellectual energy without form. After reincarnating on Earth as human beings numerous times, many of these souls come to believe that they have human shape. As a result, they lose some of their intrinsic freedom as souls. Spirits in the World of Bodhisattvas of the seventh dimension still undergo spiritual discipline in human form. Most of them only recognize themselves as human beings with two arms, two legs, a certain hairstyle, a distinctive face, and a set of clothes. They feel uncomfortable unless they have a human appearance. Although they are extremely virtuous and excellent leaders, their spiritual power is limited because they can only see themselves in human form. Tathagatas in the eighth dimension understand that they are essentially spirits without human form. For them, life on Earth is only a fragment of memories in a long process of reincarnation. They see themselves as intellectual energy, or a mass of light, and they take on this form on a daily basis.

Suppose a psychic on Earth could leave her physical body and travel to the eighth dimension. What do you think she would see? Actually, tathagatas would probably appear before her in human form, much the way they looked when they lived on Earth. They would invite her to their homes and would offer her coffee or wine, which would possess a fantastic fragrance and taste nothing like they do on Earth. When the psychic returned to this world, she would probably describe the eighth dimension as follows: "The World of Tathagatas in the eighth dimension is truly an amazing place. The inhabitants are divinely beautiful, the streets are paved with rubies, and the buildings are adorned with diamonds. Interior rooms are designed with magnificent crystal pillars, and the marble tables shimmer with beauty." Emanuel Swedenborg, the famous eighteenth-century European theologian and psychic, described his trip to the spirit world in just this way. However, someone with a higher spiritual awareness would gaze at the same scene and instead of seeing jewel-encrusted buildings and streets paved with rubies, he would see only a tathagata standing in front of him with a smile. If he looked at the tathagata more carefully, he would see only a giant ball of light. What appear to be rubies, diamonds, and other jewels only represent the world of the eighth dimension in a way that people on Earth can understand.

Inhabitants of the World of Tathagatas are aware of the fact that their true nature is energy without form. Those who have attained the enlightenment of tathagatas while living on Earth have also come to understand the spiritual law *"one is many—many are one."* In the World of Tathagatas, there is no objective way of recognizing "one." There is only absolute existence. "One" can become "ten" or "ten thousand" at the same time. Similarly, "one thousand" can be "one." The various functions of each consciousness manifest as individual entities, but only the core consciousness that integrates all these individual consciousnesses knows how many functions it has.

Let me explain this concept more simply. If a tathagata has ten tasks, it can split into ten different people to accomplish them. If it has ten thousand tasks, it can appear as ten thousand people. Even when it splits into ten thousand people, however, the master consciousness can still integrate them all and recognize itself as a single entity.

Kitarō Nishida (1870-1945), founder of the Kyōto school of philosophy, has brought this law of the eighth dimension to light after many years of philosophical study. He was originally from the World of Tathagatas, and his subconscious provided him with inspiration. In the eighth dimension, it is possible to have an "absolutely contradictory self-identity." That is to say, what appears to be diverse, and even contradictory, can be understood as one. In this way Kitarō Nishida seems to have partially expressed the enlightenment of tathagatas while he lived on Earth.

7. The Enlightenment of the Sun Realm

The awareness of "one is many—many are one" lies beyond human physical senses; to truly perceive it requires the enlightenment of tathagatas. To understand this law is to fully grasp the truth that souls are fragments of Buddha's light—conscious energy without form. Among the 45 billion souls that belong to Earth's spirit group, fewer than five hundred reside in the World of Tathagatas of the eighth dimension, virtually the highest level of enlightenment that people on Earth can achieve. It is inordinately difficult to achieve this level of enlightenment, which goes beyond such dualities as good and evil to reach the stage philosophers call "sublation," a level of integration on a higher level. You cannot achieve this spiritual wisdom solely through self-improvement and spiritual discipline. You need not just intellectual clarity, but also an extraordinary breadth of wisdom to understand the magnificent drama of the universe and to master the laws that govern it.

What kinds of people reside in the eighth dimension? Let me give you some examples of people who incarnated in Japan and returned to the eighth dimension. Taishi Shōtoku, a regent and politician of the Asuka period who incorporated Buddhism into Japan's culture and later reincarnated as Abraham Lincoln, resides in the World of Tathagatas. So does the philosopher Kitarō Nishida, who was an incarnation of Aristotle,* along with Kūkai, a monk who founded Shingon ("True Words") Buddhism.

The fewer than five hundred souls that reside in the World of Tathagatas are divided into roughly four levels. The lowest, the upper part of the Brahma Realm, is inhabited by approximately forty tathagatas. Next is the Holy Realm, home to approximately 120 souls. Above that lies the Holy Light Realm, which has about 280 inhabitants. And the highest level of the eighth dimension is known as the Sun

---

* Ryuho Okawa, *The Golden Laws.* (New York: Lantern Books, 2003).

Realm. The Sun Realm includes the Cosmic Realm of the ninth dimension, but strictly speaking, the Sun Realm lies between the eighth and ninth dimensions and is inhabited by around twenty Grand Tathagatas.

Who are the Grand Tathagatas that reside in this Sun Realm? Some of the well-known gods of Shintoism are found here, among them Ameno-minakanushi-no-kami,[6] Ameno-tokotachi-no-kami, and Kamumusuhi-no-kami. The Christian saints Augustine and Thomas Aquinas reside here, as do Taoist leaders such as Lao-tzu and Chuang-tzu. Mozi, the founder of Mohism, resides in the Sun Realm; so do the ancient Greek god Apollo and the Greek philosophers Socrates and Plato. Buddhist tathagata Ashuku Nyorai, and Yakushi Nyorai, a tathagata of medicine, both reside in the Sun Realm. Muhammad, the founder of Islam, resides in the Holy Light Realm, a realm directly below the Sun Realm.

What state of enlightenment do all these spirits in the Sun Realm have in common? These spirits are granted special status to serve as gods, and they occupy a state of mind that cannot be achieved simply through human efforts. Undergoing spiritual training as a human being on Earth will not by itself enable you to reach the level of the Sun Realm. The spirits in this realm join the ranks of the Grand Spirits, who are often revered as the foundational gods of various religions around the world.

On what grounds do I say that their level of enlightenment is beyond what you can achieve on Earth? These spirits in the Sun Realm are directly involved in planning the evolution of humanity. They facilitate religious reform; they plan, design, and create new civilizations; and they open new eras in human history. In these ways, the spirits of the Sun Realm directly help the Grand Spirits of the Cosmic Realm in the ninth dimension.

8. The Enlightenment of Shakyamuni Buddha(1): The Great Awakening

Before I describe the enlightenment of the Cosmic Realm of the ninth dimension, let me talk about what Gautama Siddhartha, or Shakyamuni Buddha, achieved in India more than two thousand years ago. At the age of twenty-nine, Gautama Siddhartha left the home of his wealthy parents in search of enlightenment. For the next six years he practiced the harsh austerity of ascetic training. Eventually he left this practice and attained great enlightenment at the age of thirty-five. This happened one night at around one o'clock, after a week of meditation. Let me describe the exact thoughts Gautama Siddhartha had at the time of his great awakening.

"For many years, I barely ate or drank. I have practiced

asceticism, believing that I could attain a great spiritual awakening by mortifying my flesh to its limit. Six years have passed since I left my wife, Yashodhara, and my son, Rahula, and fled from Kapilavastu Palace, rejecting the pleas of my father, King Suddhodana, that I succeed him to the throne. When I lived in the palace, I was strong and vigorous, adept at both military and literary arts. But look at me now. I am just skin and bone. If our purpose in life were to excoriate and torment our bodies, then what would be the point of dwelling in physical bodies at all? If the Eternal Buddha* wished for human beings to deny the flesh, wouldn't that imply that those who commit suicide are the most enlightened ones?

"But what is the benefit of suicide? According to the universal law of cause and effect, if we create seeds of suffering by committing suicide, then suffering is what we'll reap. The state of enlightenment is a state of tranquility, but how can we possibly attain such peace of mind through the torments of asceticism? Torturing my physical body this way is none other than a way to kill myself, and this is not a way to enlightenment. The only result I have achieved through this practice is an attitude of severity. My eyes are passing harsh judgments and show no love or mercy. How can I be truly

---

* The term, "Eternal Buddha" refers to Lord El Cantare and denotes the spiritual father of Shakyamuni Buddha.

kind and compassionate if I can't find peace of mind or fill my own heart with happiness?

"What exactly is the happiness that I can find within myself? When I lived as a prince in Kapilavastu Palace, I had all the money, women, and luxuries that I could ask for. But was my heart filled with happiness? No, my monotonous life was filled with languor. My heart was empty, and my mind was racked by conflicts, inflamed by other people's desires and intentions. Had I inherited the throne, it would have been my duty to lead my people to war against neighboring countries, causing terrible bloodshed and death.

"A life lived in pursuit of worldly status and fame can only bring hollowness. My life in Kapilavastu Palace was not a life of true happiness. I felt spiritually unfulfilled, and I lived in constant anxiety and frustration. We find true happiness not in stagnation and laziness, but in daily spiritual progress. Happiness is found not in worldly success, but in the improvement of our souls and the refinement of our divine nature. We children of the Eternal Buddha experience true happiness when we improve ourselves according to His Will.

"As children of the Eternal Buddha, we can find the path to enlightenment and true happiness neither in the extravagant life of royalty nor in the strictures of ascetic training; we can find peace of mind neither in hedonistic excess nor the harshest privation. The right way of living for human beings is to abandon both extremes and to seek the Truths in the Middle Way. Only when we live a balanced life can we find the Middle Way.

"What we truly seek as human beings is a life of perfect harmony. We can create a world of perfect harmony, a kingdom of Heaven, within our mind when we abandon the extremes of pain and pleasure, enter the Middle Way, and practice the Eightfold Path of Right View, Right Thought, Right Speech, Right Action, Right Livelihood, Right Effort, Right Mindfulness, and Right Concentration. When all of us do this, the kingdom of Heaven will appear on Earth.

"Thus, true happiness is to be found in experiencing joy and making spiritual progress in our daily lives. We can increase this spiritual joy by understanding and mastering the Eightfold Path."

9. The Enlightenment of Shakyamuni Buddha(2): Entering Nirvana

As I describe what was in Shakyamuni's mind when he attained great enlightenment, I find myself reliving his experience of 2,500 years ago. It feels as if I could easily devote an entire book to this topic, which might be a worthy undertaking at another time, but for now I will skip over forty-five years of Shakyamuni's life to the day he was passing away at the age of eighty. Under sal trees in Kushinagar, Shakyamuni Buddha lay on his right side, his right arm folded under his head and his left hand holding his ailing stomach. In his last moments, he could hardly speak. Some disciples whose spiritual hearts were open were able to hear Shakyamuni's inner voice and later recorded his message in the Nirvana Sutra. Now let me recall and convey his inner thoughts at that time. As Shakyamuni entered Nirvana, his thoughts turned to his life and his disciples.

"Since I attained the great enlightenment at the age of thirty-five, I have sought goodness and taught the Truths. But now the time has come for me to bid farewell to my physical body. Everything in this world is transient, and I have no attachment to this material form. For forty-five years I have been able to teach people the path to enlightenment and show them the right way to live as human beings. My true essence is the Laws, the Dharma I have taught.

"I must thank you, my disciples, for attending to my personal needs over the years and for helping to spread the Laws. Thanks to your efforts, my order has grown to more than five thousand monks and nuns, and there are hundreds of thousands of lay followers throughout India. Even in the face of religious persecution, you have continued to spread the Laws. For this I am eternally grateful to you, and ask only that after I am gone, you will keep working as diligently as before.

"Sariputra, you passed away several years ago, but I look

forward to seeing you again, and enjoying another of our talks, knee to knee. You were such a great help to me. As the 'best in wisdom,' you were always a good listener, and made it easy for me to preach. Sometimes your seemingly silly questions made me smile, but other listeners who didn't have the courage to ask questions appreciated yours very much.

"Mahamaudgalyayana, although I knew it was part of your spiritual discipline, I was unable to hold back my tears when I heard that you who were known as the 'best in divine supernatural powers' had been murdered by misguided religious zealots. I can see you approaching, riding on a shining cloud, to accompany me to Heaven.

"Mahakatyayana, you who were the 'best in debate' were always able to explain my teachings in a way that others could understand. Continue to sow the seeds of the Dharma in remote areas after I am gone. Go and spread my teachings in West India, beginning with the Avanti region.

"Subhuti, you who were the 'best in understanding the emptiness' never allowed yourself to become attached to material things, and gained a deep understanding of my teachings of the emptiness and egolessness. Continue your diligent efforts.

"Aniruddha, I once admonished you in an unusually strong tone because you fell asleep during one of my talks. In penance you meditated night and day, until you lost your eyesight. Fortunately, you have learned to see through your spiritual eyes, becoming known as the 'best in clairvoyance.' You were once so young and innocent, but now I can see your hair turning gray.

"Purnamaitrayaniputra, as a member of the Shakya clan, you were always clever, the 'best in preaching the Dharma.' You and the other Purna, who plans to travel west to spread my teachings, will become rivals in the best sense.

"Mahakasyapa, you will not be able to witness my passing and will arrive here a week late. You will be furious with Ananda, who carelessly served me poisonous mushrooms and so hastened my departure from this world. You will try to expel him from the order and will weep bitterly over my death. You who were known as the 'best in ascetic disciplines' were always meticulous about the methods of religious practice. After my death, however, I encourage you to do away with petty rules and restrictions.

"Upali, you were the 'best in observing the precepts.' You have always done your work with care, and you were courteous to everybody you met. Although you were from a lower caste, you remained undaunted and devoted yourself to spiritual discipline among others who were born aristocrats. I am proud of you.

"Rahula, although you were my son, you practiced spiritual discipline privately under Sariputra. As a result, you were called the 'best in esoteric training.' Sadly, you left this world early. You were expected to succeed me, and it was unfortunate to lose you so soon. I could not do anything for you as a father, but I hope you are living happily in Heaven.

"Jivaka, celebrated doctor, you have cured my illnesses numerous times, but this time even your skills are not sufficient to heal me. All things are transient. Just as you cannot stop the flow of a river, you cannot extend my life on Earth any longer.

"When I think of you, my beloved disciples, I can't stop thinking about what will happen to you after I am gone. Remember this: although I will be leaving this world shortly, my teachings remain on Earth to be passed on for thousands of years for the nourishment of people's souls. Always keep this in mind, my disciples. My life is like the full moon in the sky. Even when it is covered by clouds and disappears from your sight, it continues to cast its light. Like the moon, my life shines forever. Life is eternal.

"After I am gone, use the teachings I have given you over the past forty-five years as food for your souls. Live according to my teachings, and let them light the path. Instead of relying on others, keep the torch of Dharma burning within you, and use it to illuminate the way ahead. Stand up firmly and walk steadily.

"Make yourself your torchlight, and live according to the Laws I have taught you. They will help you improve your souls and save others' souls. My disciples, these are my last words: All things in this world will pass. Complete your spiritual work without neglecting it."

These were the final thoughts of Shakyamuni Buddha as he entered Nirvana.

10. *The Enlightenment of the Ninth Dimension*

Shakyamuni attained the highest level of enlightenment that a human being can achieve, surpassing the enlightenment that Jesus Christ achieved. Unfortunately, however, Shakyamuni Buddha was unable to pass on what he understood of the Truths of the great universe even in the forty-five years he devoted to teaching his disciples. Hardly any of his disciples were able to attain the enlightenment of tathagatas while they were on Earth, so most of them were unable to understand the Truths of the Creation of the great universe and its multidimensional structure. Because in those days India was disrupted by war, Shakyamuni realized that he would not be able to save people's souls by teaching the cosmic laws. So he decided to lower his sights and focus on raising people's awareness to the level of arhat through his teachings of the Eightfold Path.

To attain the enlightenment of the ninth dimension, you must fulfill the following three conditions.

I. You must have a full and complete understanding of the Truths and be able to preach them in a way that is appropriate for people of all spiritual levels.

2. You must have a full understanding of the genesis, or Creation, and of the history of the universe and our planet Earth.

3. You must have a full understanding of the laws governing the multidimensional universe, which begins with the fourth dimension and extends far beyond.

In terms of the first condition, Shakyamuni excelled at preaching the Truths in a way that was well suited to each listener. As for the second condition, he gained a complete understanding of the genesis when he attained great enlightenment under the Bodhi tree and had a mystical experience of his spirit body becoming one with the great universe. He fulfilled the third condition by possessing knowledge of the laws of the universe and of the spirit world, which he expressed through his teachings of the law of cause and effect and the law of karma.

With the enlightenment of the ninth dimension comes complete mastery of the six divine supernatural powers, as well as the ability to see through past, present, and future. Shakyamuni quickly realized the danger of seekers becoming deeply enamored of supernatural powers. In order to lead by example, Shakyamuni rarely used his own spiritual powers, with the exception of mind reading.

In chapter I, I mentioned that there are ten Great Guiding Spirits of Light who have attained the enlightenment of the ninth dimension. Here is a list of their roles and responsibilities:*

MAJOR HEAVEN

I. Shakyamuni (El Cantare)
    The highest Grand Spirit of the Earth's spirit group, responsible for the creation of new ages and the building of new civilizations.

2. Jesus Christ (Amor)
    Responsible for guiding Heaven by determining its directions and policies.

3. Confucius (Therabim)
    Responsible for planning the evolution of the Earth's spirit group and interacting with other star clusters.

4. Manu (Achemene)
    Responsible for dealing with ethnic issues.

---

* As of 1994.

5. Maitrayer (Orgon)

    Responsible for dispersing, refracting, and reflecting Buddha's light.

6. Newton (Kaitron)

    In charge of science and technology.

7. Zeus (Theoria)

    In charge of the arts, such as music, fine arts, and literature.

8. Zoroaster (Samatria)

    In charge of moral perfection.

MINOR HEAVEN

9. Moses (Moria)

    Chief Commander of the forces dedicated to the dissolution of Hell; also in charge of miraculous phenomena.

10. Enlil

    A god of disaster and vengeance who sends guidance to the Sorcery Realm of Arabia, the Yoga Realm of India, the Sennin Realm of China, and the Sennin and Tengu Realms of Japan.

Since the core consciousness of El Cantare currently resides on Earth, Jesus Christ primarily acts as the senior decision maker in the ninth dimension on behalf of El Cantare. Jesus himself is scheduled to descend to Earth about four hundred years from now. By then, the southern half of North America will have sunk beneath the ocean, and a new continent, New Atlantis, which will connect directly to Canada, will have risen out of the ocean in the Bermuda Triangle area. Jesus is currently scheduled to reincarnate on New Atlantis, where he is expected to preach the Truths based on the principles of love and justice for the new space age.

In this chapter, I have described the various levels of enlightenment up to the ninth dimension. Of course, a higher level of enlightenment can be seen in the consciousnesses of the tenth dimension. But the three planetary consciousnesses in the tenth dimension—Sun Consciousness, Moon Consciousness, and Earth Consciousness—are not human spirits. If we want to understand enlightenment as it relates to human beings, then we don't have to delve into the enlightenment of the tenth dimension. Nevertheless, I would just add that the enlightenment of the tenth dimension is a state in which all human elements have been removed. In other words, the planetary consciousnesses in the tenth dimension are large spheres of light with a sense of purpose.

THE GOLDEN AGES:
THE HISTORY OF
HUMANKIND

1. Heralding a New Humankind

We have already entered the twenty-first century, and many people today look towards this new stage of humankind with both excitement and anxiety. What could be awaiting us in this new era? What events will unfold? What will the people be like, and who will be our leaders? There are many signs lying right within today's society that answer these questions and herald the coming of the new era and a new civilization. We are currently living in a time of transition, a time when the old will crumble away and the new will boldly emerge. The new era is already flowering all around us, and it is the mission of a prophet to point out these developments and portents to his contemporaries.

Any thoughtful discussion of the present and the future must be based on an understanding of the past, much of which has been hidden by the mists of time or mistaken for myth. Approximately ten thousand years ago, the ancient world witnessed the violent end of the advanced civilization of Atlantis, which was swallowed up by the ocean. But in the long march of civilizations, when one declines, another always emerges. In time, a new people rose and flourished in Egypt. Egyptian culture spread and formed many societies in countries and regions all around the world, including Persia, Judea, China, Europe, America, and Japan. The most notable quality of this civilization is its emphasis on using intelligence to understand the world. We could call this the civilization of intelligence, which came to a close at the end of the twentieth century.

The civilization of Atlantis, on the other hand, was based on reason. Both the Grand Tathagata Maitrayer and Koot Hoomi of the Cosmic World of the ninth dimension played major roles in the development of Atlantis. (Koot Hoomi is better known as Archimedes and as his later incarnation, Sir Isaac Newton.)

The civilization of Atlantis was preceded by another unique civilization, Mu, which flourished on a continent of the same name in the Pacific Ocean some fifteen thousand years ago. The Mu civilization was characterized by the use of light energy. The people of Mu had made great advancements in scientific and spiritual research into the energy found in light. They also focused greatly on learning how to increase the amount and power of their own individual light energy.

Approximately twenty-seven thousand years ago, prior to the Mu civilization, a civilization flourished on the continent of Lamudia,* a landmass located in today's Indian Ocean. The people of this civilization concentrated on the development of sensitivity. Whereas El Cantare (Shakyamuni Buddha) was closely involved in shaping the civilization of Mu, the ninth-dimension spirits Manu and Zeus played central roles in the development of Lamudia. Here, the main goal of people's learning and training was to develop sensitivity; the most adept Lamudians were capable of distinguishing three thousand different colors and 2,500 fragrances.

Even further back in history, the Earth used to rotate on a different axis, and the continent of Antarctica had a temperate climate with a slightly different shape. It was called Myutram and was the site of a flourishing civilization that disappeared 153,000 years ago. Unlike Mu or Atlantis, this

---

* As some scholars confuse Lemuria with the continent of Mu, I have used the name Lamudia in this edition, which was used commonly at the time this civilization existed.

continent did not sink into the sea. When the Earth's axis shifted to what it is today, the continent's position moved in such a way that the climate became untenable for virtually all forms of life. This shift marked the start of the famous Ice Age. As we will one day discover, many traces of this civilization are still preserved beneath Antarctica's perennial ice.

An even more ancient people called the Garna created a civilization characterized by its focus on developing psychic and supernatural powers. At that time, approximately 735,000 years ago, what are now the African and South American continents were still one unbroken landmass called Garna.* Its people faced destruction when this massive continent was jolted by massive tectonic movements beneath the earth. Garna split into two landmasses, which began to move in opposite directions. A gigantic earthquake, which today would register a magnitude of ten or more on the Richter scale, completed the total destruction of this civilization.

What I have described here is not science fiction or myth. These are true accounts from Earth's long history. I convey this knowledge to you and to all the people of this present age, as well as future ones, because it provides a valuable context for considering our civilization today and provides

---

* I have used *Garna* in this edition, a name that was used during the time of the Garna civilization, to avoid confusion with the supercontinent Gondwana. Garna and Gondwana are different in their sizes and the ages in which they existed.

insight into how we should shape and understand the civilizations of the future. With that in mind, I'd like to devote this chapter to taking a closer look at the most significant developments of our rich past.

2. The Garna Civilization

In the four-hundred-million-year history of humankind, countless civilizations have emerged, flourished, and vanished like frothy bubbles in a turbulent river. For the purposes of people today, I don't need to explore this history in too much detail, but I will share with you the parts that are most valuable and necessary for our understanding of present and future societies. There is enormous wisdom to be found in examining these great civilizations of the past. For this reason, I will open the pages of the Akashic record, the complete archive of the world's history kept in the spirit world, and offer you a brief account of the major civilizations of the last million years, starting with Garna.

The continent of Garna was formed 962,000 years ago after a massive underwater volcanic eruption caused the seabed to rise and form a landmass between present-day Africa and South America. Four civilizations rose and fell on the continent of Garna, but here I will focus only on the final one, which flourished for approximately twenty-five thousand years beginning around 760,000 years ago, until the civilization was destroyed by the tectonic shift described earlier.

The people of Garna were very tall; on average, men measured 2.1 meters in height (six feet eleven inches), and women 1.8 meters (five feet eleven inches). Interestingly, the men of Garna had a third eye, located in the center of their foreheads, approximately two centimeters (almost an inch) above the eyebrows. This eye was usually closed, but it opened when its psychic powers were required. Women did not possess a third eye, and as a result were subjugated by men.

According to the Garnian folktale, which survived until the last years of Garna, God created men and women as equals. As proof of that, God gave men a third eye to allow them to protect themselves and their kin, while He gave women the womb so their kin might prosper. A Garnian woman's womb possessed psychic powers that allowed her not only to bear children but also to communicate with her future children in the spirit world. Women of Garna chose to become pregnant only after communicating with their future progeny and after both sides agreed to the pregnancy. So unlike in our times, abortion was never an issue.

In Garna, eight tribes fought constantly for supremacy, so people needed to protect themselves from outside enemies all the time. The men's third eye acted as a weapon, and its color varied depending on the tribe; it could be yellow, green, purple, black, gray, or brown. The degree to which each tribe's supernatural abilities were developed also varied. Although the principal forms of their supernatural powers had physical effects, some tribes focused on developing precognition. They could foretell enemy attacks.

Unfortunately, the importance of refining the mind was not part of the teachings of this people. Garnians were mainly concerned with the *type* of psychic powers they wanted to attain through their training. As a result, when the people of Garna perished and returned to the spirit world, many of them went to Minor Heaven, which is inhabited by *sennin* (hermit wizards), *tengu* (long-nosed wizards), and sorcerers of all kinds.

Once Garna vanished from Earth, no other civilization would possess a third eye. However, the concept of the chakra (spiritual power center) on the forehead, which is part of the yogic and tantric traditions, can be traced back to the third eye of Garna's people.

3. The Myutram Civilization

As mentioned earlier, the civilization of Garna came to an abrupt end after the catastrophic split of the continent. One autumn evening approximately 735,000 years ago, the earth shook and gave a thunderous roar as a massive crack suddenly appeared, running from north to south right through the center of Ecarna, one of Garna's major cities. At first, the crack was a hundred kilometers (sixty-two miles) long, but seawater quickly surged in. The second stage of the disaster came three days later, when a magnitude-ten earthquake shook the land. This earthquake's epicenter was located right below the city. Ecarna's entire population of three hundred thousand perished this day. The crack continued to grow to a length of several thousand kilometers until the continent eventually split completely in two. The two halves drew further apart until, tens of thousands of years later, they became situated into the geographical locations of present-day Africa and South America.

But in a southeastern city called Emilna, there was a group of people who were particularly skilled in foretelling the future. Thanks to their precognition skills, some of them were able to foresee this catastrophe. They escaped by ship and successfully fled to an uninhabited continent to the south (this was one of the events that inspired the story of Noah's Ark). However, the Emilna people lost the advanced tools they once had, as well as many of their leaders. As a result, they gradually regressed into a simple agrarian-based culture. They even lost their ability to use the third eye, and over time, the eye itself disappeared completely under the pressures of evolution.

On this new continent, which was named Myutram,

many civilizations emerged and disappeared, but the most significant one by far took on the name of the continent, and flourished between 300,000 and 153,000 years ago. The landmass of present-day Antarctica comprises about 80 percent of the original continent of Myutram. The orientation of the Earth's rotational axis was different in the days of the Myutram civilization, and this region was blessed with a temperate climate. Grain very similar to wheat thrived in their climate and soil, and became the basis of Myutram's agriculture.

In fact, what particularly distinguished the Myutram civilization was the central role that agriculture and knowledge of food played in the culture. The Myutram studied all kinds of food extensively in hopes of discovering what combinations of foods were most beneficial to humans, in terms of both health and character development. They carefully studied the relationship between particular culinary lifestyles and inner life. They researched just about every aspect of food—what food should be served to cultivate a gentle disposition, what kinds of fish improve people's reflexes, which dairy products should be consumed in what amounts and how often to extend the human lifespan, what type of alcohol has a positive effect on brain activity, and so on. The Myutram trained specialists in all aspects of their food culture, and people would study hard from a young age to become professionals in specific food-related fields. They had professors in many fields, including enhancing longevity, increasing stamina, and improving memory.

The Myutram civilization produced a large volume of research on the relationship between eating habits and temperament. In contrast to the people of Garna, who despite an aggressive nature placed a high value on spiritual powers, the people of Myutram were peace-loving but tended to undervalue spirituality. Signs of modern-day materialism could already be seen in Myutram culture. Although this civilization's discoveries of the relationship between food and human temperament were noteworthy, by focusing too much on food, Myutram culture neglected humankind's true mission—to study and train the soul in order to promote its growth.

Many people today who take a special interest in food and nutrition most likely had numerous reincarnations in the Myutram civilization, which reached its peak around 160,000 years ago when the ninth-dimension spirit Moria incarnated on Earth as a great spiritual leader named Emula. He initiated a grand-scale spiritual revolution based on the teaching that humankind needed to shift "from a food-based life to a life based on the mind," but he was persecuted harshly for undermining Myutram's traditional values. Although his movement was unsuccessful, Moria did succeed in imprinting upon people's minds that there were forces beyond food that shaped human temperament. In this respect, what

Emula tried to accomplish was a forerunner of modern religious movements that have fought against materialism.

Then, 153,000 years ago, a sudden pole shift occurred, and the surface of the continent of Myutram froze over, triggering what we know as the Ice Age.

4. The Lamudia Civilization

The sudden change in the Earth's axis was the direct cause of Myutram's end. One evening during sunset, people looked upon the sky to find it a ghastly red. The entire sky looked as if it had been drenched in blood. A deluge of inquiries flooded the civilization's leading scientists, but no one could provide an answer. Then, at around ten o'clock that night, all the stars began to fall from the sky. People soon realized that the Earth itself had begun to spin the way a ball under water rotates when it shoots up to the surface. The Earth had flipped itself over.

Within months of this phenomenon, snow began to fall on the once temperate lands of Myutram, and the ground began to freeze over. This sounded the death knell for Myutram, although its people put up a fierce fight against starvation. Some even created underground cities in order to survive, but even these would disappear within three years.

Unfortunately, the rainy season had just started. This

time, the heavy rains fell as snow, and in less than two weeks, the ground was covered by more than five meters (over sixteen feet) of snow. The capital city, La Myute, was destroyed, although some inhabitants managed to escape on ships, allowing part of the Myutram civilization to take root on a new continent.

At that time there were no large continents in the region that is now the Indian Ocean, but a small island about twice the size of Japan did exist. Several thousand refugees from Myutram settled there, and their numbers grew over time. Around eighty-six thousand years ago, this island suddenly began to rise up from the sea, lifted by a massive expanse of land that emerged from the ocean. In just a year's time, this landmass had grown into the massive continent that would become known as Lamudia. Shaped like a diamond, it stretched 3,500 kilometers (2,200 miles) from east to west and 4,700 kilometers (2,900 miles) from north to south. Vegetation grew in abundance on the fertile soils that developed on this continent.

About forty-four thousand years ago, a spirit who would later incarnate in Greece as the ninth-dimension spirit Zeus was born in Lamudia. His name was Elemaria. A man of exceptional holiness, Elemaria was a genius in all aspects of art, including literature, fine arts, and music. Through art, the great saint Elemaria taught people the joy of living and the glory of God, and as a result, music, painting, literature, poetry, architecture, and sculpture attained previously unknown heights in the Lamudia civilization. Many who excel in the arts today may have learned their skills in a previous life in Lamudia.

About twenty-nine thousand years ago, after the incarnation of the great saint Elemaria, another ninth-dimension spirit was born. This spirit, called Manu, was given the name Margarit. His name meant "one who rises to compete" and had two implications. First, his greatness rivaled that of Elemaria, who had been worshipped as the people's almighty god. Second, he was the first person to introduce competition into the arts.

Margarit also served to bring an enormous light to Lamudia, and as a mark of respect, he was often called Great Master Margarit. Margarit taught that God is ultimately found in the greatest expression of art. He divided his people into tribes according to five different fields of the arts—music, painting, literature, architecture, and craftsmanship—and encouraged all to strive for perfection. Every three years he held competitions to determine which tribe had produced the finest art, and the winning tribe was given the prize of being the country's ruling class until the next competition.

This system of selecting rulers through fair public contests became the forerunner of modern democracy. Because he saw God in great art and rewarded great artists with lead-

ership positions, he created the foundations for a form of rule
that combined religion and government.

5. The Mu Civilization

The end of the Lamudian civilization came quite abruptly
twenty-seven thousand years ago on a blistering hot summer
afternoon, when people were euphorically enjoying one of
their favorite pastimes: listening to exquisite Lamudian
music. It was common practice among Lamudians to enjoy
music for two hours every afternoon, and it was during this
time that catastrophe struck. Chandeliers began to sway violently, and glass windows shattered. In a matter of minutes,
Lamudia's magnificent modern concert halls were collapsing
as the eastern portion of the continent began to sink into the
ocean.

By four o'clock in the afternoon, half the continent had
already disappeared. By seven o'clock the following morning,
only a vast expanse of shimmering blue ocean welcomed the
rising sun. Not a trace of the continent could be found except
the remains of the Lamudians above the ocean. The destruction of Lamudia was swift and complete; its entire population of 2.5 million vanished into the sea. (In catastrophic
disasters, people are affected without regard to whether they
are wicked or virtuous.) However, the civilization itself sur-

vived, for the Lamudians had established a colony on a continent named Moa, which later came to be known as Mu.

The continent of Mu, which was located in the Pacific Ocean, had emerged some 370,000 years ago, and had existed longer than Lamudia. Mu's shape changed through time, and at the end of the Lamudian civilization, it was approximately twice the area of present-day Australia and was situated where Indonesia is found today. Although people had lived on this continent for hundreds of thousands of years, they did not yet have an advanced form of civilization. Most of the northern inhabitants were fishers, those in the south were hunters, and those in the midwest were farmers.

The more advanced people of Lamudia eventually invaded the Mu people. Around twenty-eight thousand years ago, the Lamudians sent a large fleet to the Mu continent and began to colonize it by force. They captured Mu people and took them back to Lamudia as slaves. While Lamudians spent their days enjoying the arts and studying, their Mu slaves toiled away at the day-to-day tasks of life. This caused massive clouds of dark thought-energy to form over the Lamudian civilization, which eventually resulted in the complete destruction of the continent. However, since some of the advanced culture of Lamudia had taken root in the colony of Mu, after Lamudia vanished, a new advanced civilization slowly but surely began to appear in the land of Mu.

About twenty-thousand years ago, Escallent, who later

reincarnated as the ninth-dimension spirit Zoroaster, descended to the land of Mu. (The name *Escallent* means "excellent" and is the original source of that word.) He put great emphasis on scientific applications of the power of sunlight, which he believed was important in two ways. He regarded light as both a holy emanation of God's glory and as a form of energy that could be harnessed to provide useful power. Escallent taught people to put their hands together in a sign of respect and to bow on one knee whenever they saw a source of light, whether it was the sun, the moon, or an indoor lamp. This became the basis of later Asian traditions, including the custom of bowing.

How did Escallent make light useful? Fortunately, he was receiving guidance from Koot Hoomi in Heaven, whose later incarnations as Archimedes and Isaac Newton are well known today. He was also receiving help from Enlil, who possessed a scientific mind. Guided by these spirits, Escallent focused on amplifying the power of light. This was the first time humankind had begun to establish an age of science.

Escallent inspired scientists and engineers to create gigantic solar energy amplifiers, which his people used to light their rooms, drive their ships, and run factories. At the center of every Mu city was a silver pyramid whose sides measured thirty meters (one hundred feet). These pyramids absorbed sunlight and amplified its energy before transmitting it to smaller pyramids measuring ten meters (thirty feet) on each side, located in the city's smaller districts. These pyramids in turn transferred the solar energy to even smaller pyramids, with sides measuring one meter (three feet), which were mounted on the rooftops of every house. This system of advanced solar technology became known as pyramid power and was passed down to the next civilization, Atlantis.

6. *The Age of La Mu*

The civilization of Mu reached its peak approximately seventeen thousand years ago, during the reign of ninth-dimension spirit King La Mu. Worship of the sun and the development of solar technology were at an all-time high when he incarnated onto Earth with the name La Mu, which meant "the Great King, the Light of Mu." An earlier incarnation of Shakyamuni Buddha, King La Mu ruled a vast empire. The former continent of Moa was renamed in his honor, and from that time on, its civilization and the continent itself would be known by the name Mu. A large metropolitan city of this empire, La Mu, was also named after him.

With the Mu civilization making great strides in science and technology, King La Mu felt that there was no better opportunity to build a kingdom of God on Earth. La Mu's vast spiritual powers gave him the ability to freely converse with the holy spirits of Heaven whenever he wished. Amor, who would later be born on Earth as Jesus Christ, was one of the principal spirits who protected La Mu from his place in Heaven.

La Mu's teachings were based on three principal creeds. First, all people of Mu must understand that God is like the sun. God, like the sun, is radiating brilliance and constantly shining His light on all of us on Earth. Second, all people of Mu must emulate the sun's love and compassion. The essence of love and compassion is to fill the hearts of all those around us with light. Third, all people of Mu must always strive to grow, not only by developing our artistic, intellectual, and physical abilities, but also by advancing ourselves spiritually. La Mu's teachings became the first form of religion, established seventeen thousand years ago.

It's easy to tell from this history that the teachings of Shakyamuni Buddha were already taking root on Earth in La Mu's age. And in fact, fourteen thousand years after La Mu's death, he would reincarnate in India as Shakyamuni Buddha and become the founder of one of the world's greatest religions. During La Mu's reign, religion and politics were not separated as they are today. The highest form of religion was considered the best form of government, and the greatest religious leader was also the greatest civic leader. This makes perfect sense; since all human beings were born from God, people who are closest to God would be best suited to govern the spiritual lives of His people, and because God is close at hand, this person would also make an outstanding ruler.

Every night, La Mu would go to his temple and kneel in meditation as he discussed important matters of state with the Divine Spirits. This practice should be the basis for running all governments. Since politics is the art of governing an entire people, the blunders of politicians affect not only themselves but also all other citizens. Politicians' actions can affect whether people will live or die, and can even lead people's souls on a downward path. If politics is based purely on human perceptions, it could become the domain of arrogance. As La Mu knew, the essence of effective politics lies in humbling yourself, calming your mind, clearing it of all thoughts of the self, and listening to the words of God. This was the true start and basis of politics and the art of governing.

After La Mu passed away, his people forgot the essence of his great teachings, and the Mu civilization began to decline. What's more, people began to deny the power of enlightenment, and a sinister worship of animal spirits began to spread. This rise of a dangerous spiritual power caused many people to scorn the valuable teachings of love and compassion, and created dark clouds of negative energy that spread across the whole continent.

As a result, approximately 15,300 years ago, the continent of Mu began to sink in three stages beneath the waves of the Pacific Ocean. Needless to say, the large and advanced city of La Mu disappeared along with the rest of the continent. However, once again, some inhabitants were able to escape by ship. Those who headed north became ancestors of the Vietnamese, Japanese, and Chinese. Others who traveled east across the Pacific Ocean came to inhabit the Andes region in South America. A third group of people journeyed in search of a new world and eventually discovered the continent of Atlantis.

7. The Atlantis Civilization

The continent of Atlantis was home to the great civilization of Atlantis, which immediately preceded our own time. It was situated in the Atlantic Ocean, in the area known today as the Bermuda Triangle. Originally a small island no larger than Great Britain, Atlantis grew following an eruption beneath the sea seventy-five thousand years ago. People first started to inhabit the landmass about forty-two thousand years ago. These first inhabitants were primitive tribal people who came from neighboring islands.

Signs of a new civilization began to appear on this continent approximately sixteen thousand years ago, a few hundred years before the Mu continent sank. It was at this time that Koot Hoomi, the ninth-dimension spirit who later reincarnated in Greece as the great scientist Archimedes, was born to bring civilization to people who had until then lived mainly by fishing and hunting.

Koot Hoomi was fascinated by the mysterious power found in plant life. He wanted to know why seeds are able to sprout, grow, create leaves, and bloom. He spent twenty years studying these things, trying to find out how a stem could grow out of a bulb, and eventually discovered that when life changes form, it initiates a huge conversion of energy. This was indeed a discovery of the true nature of the power hidden within life: life itself is a form of energy. Koot Hoomi thought that if he could extract the energy from this conversion, it could be used as a power source. He spent the next decade searching for a way to extract this energy, and eventually, he succeeded.

Koot Hoomi's discovery shined new light on this continent and became the driving force of cultural growth. Power produced by life energy was used much the way electricity is used today. For example, the window ledges of every house were lined with rows of flasks containing flower bulbs. Each of these bulbs was connected to a machine by a special kind of wire made of nickel and chromium. The wire trapped and stored the energy that the bulb produced for its germination and growth. Another machine amplified this energy, generating enough power to support the entire household and run all its appliances.

Fifteen thousand three hundred years ago, some survivors from Mu made their way to Atlantis. Among them were scientists who knew the secrets of Mu's pyramid power and offered this knowledge to the inhabitants of their new homeland. Around this time, the Grand Tathagata Maitrayer incarnated in Atlantis as a spiritual leader named Cusanus. Saint Cusanus preached a form of deism that combined pyramid power and sun worship; he taught that everything rational and scientific is in accordance with God's Will. The best example of this, Cusanus taught, was sunlight. "How wonderful sunlight is," he said. "Not only does it benefit people scientifically through pyramid power, but it also teaches us about God's mind."

The civilization of Atlantis reached its peak approximately twelve thousand years ago under the leadership of Thoth, also known as the Omniscient and Omnipotent Lord. Thoth was a genius who excelled in many fields—including religion, politics, philosophy, science, and art—and therefore established a multi-faceted culture. A great leader, he was particularly gifted in scientific insight, and as a result, Atlantis was able to surpass even the technology of the Mu civilization, manufacturing airships and submarines driven by pyramid power.

The airships of Atlantis looked like flying whales; they were thirty meters (one hundred feet) long and four meters (thirteen feet) in diameter. The upper half of a craft was filled with gas to make it float, while the lower part carried about twenty passengers. On the roof were mounted three silver pyramids that looked like dorsal fins, which converted solar energy into power that drove the propeller attached at the rear. This meant that the airships of Atlantis could fly only on sunny days; when it rained, all air service was suspended.

The submarines of Atlantis were made of a special alloy shaped to resemble killer whales. These submarines were twenty meters (sixty-five feet) long and four meters (thirteen feet) wide. The orca was the symbol of Atlantis, and although some claim that the nation was named after a king named Atlas, the word *atlantis* means "shining golden orca." Atlantis's submarines were also fitted with three pyramids on the roof that, from a distance, resembled the dorsal fins of an orca. From time to time, they would surface to recharge their batteries with solar energy before diving again. In these various ways and many more, science and its products flourished in Atlantis.

8. The Age of Agasha

After the great Thoth passed away, science began to dominate the society because succeeding leaders were not as multifaceted as Thoth. A trend of overvaluing science developed, prompting an opposing position that advancements in science do not always produce results that accord with God's Will, and that perhaps God would want people to care about more than just science. Various religious reform movements sprang up, and Atlantis saw many people preaching and debating different ideas about how we humans should live in this world. This period, which lasted for about a thousand years, came to be known as the "age of a hundred schools of thought."

Atlantis began to slowly sink around this time, approximately eleven thousand years ago. First, the eastern third of the continent disappeared into the sea. Three hundred years later, the western third also slipped beneath the waves. Eventually, only the central third of the continent remained above sea level, but the Empire continued to thrive.

About 10,400 years ago (8,400 BCE), a man named Agasha was born in Pontis, the continent's capital city. At that time, Pontis had a population of around seven hundred thousand and had been ruled by the Amanda clan for many generations. Born into the royal Amanda clan with the given name Amon, at the age of twenty-four, the young prince was crowned king and changed his name to Agasha, which means "he who houses wisdom." He was in fact an earlier incarnation of Jesus Christ.

Like La Mu, King Agasha was both a great religious leader and a skilled political leader. In his palace, he too had a thirty-meter-high (one hundred-foot-high) golden temple shaped like a pyramid, where the young king fulfilled his religious duties. A unique aspect of his reign was that once a month, he would gather more than a hundred thousand people in a large square in the city and preach to them using a device much like today's wireless microphones.

Agasha's teachings were based on love, much like those he later preached as Jesus. Although his topics varied, he always conveyed the same basic messages:

1. The true nature of God is love, and the love in our hearts and minds is proof that human beings are children of God.
2. To practice love, first love God our Lord, then love your neighbors, who are part of God, and finally love yourself, God's servant.
3. At least once a day, pray quietly on your own and communicate with your guardian spirit and Guiding Spirits.
4. Your greatness is measured by the quality, not quantity, of the love that you give, so improve the quality of your love.

Agasha's teachings were admirable, and he was deeply revered by his people. However, a group of people who were still devoted to the deist teachings of Saint Cuzanus (Maitrayer) regarded Agasha as an enemy and plotted to kill him. For whereas Saint Cuzanus had placed great emphasis on science, logic, and a rational God, Agasha preached love and spoke of guardian spirits and Guiding Spirits, which were the antithesis of scientific logic. Those who were still devoted to Saint Cuzanus's teachings wanted to preserve the traditional values of Atlantis and mistook Agasha's teachings for beliefs that could lead people astray. There is no doubt that Agasha was a man of noble character who garnered the respect of everyone. However, a belief in the ultimate power of science was deeply entrenched in most citizens of Atlantis, so they couldn't accept Agasha's teachings about the existence of invisible guardian spirits and Guiding Spirits.

Eventually, the deists instigated a revolt, captured Agasha and the royal family, and buried them alive in the city square. This action mirrors what we've seen at the end of the twentieth century: the Truths were revealed to the people, which triggered various forms of evil to rise in defiance.

During this violent massacre on Atlantis, only one member of the royal family, Amon II, Agasha's first son, was able to escape in an airship and flee to Egypt. There, he taught people to worship the sun, and is remembered to this day as Amon-Ra. The Egyptian pyramids we see today were the results of knowledge brought by Amon II.

Many angels of light born on Earth were executed during the deist rebellion, and for a time, it seemed that devils had triumphed in Atlantis. Their victory, however, would be short lived. The dark clouds of evil thought-energy that had spread throughout the land caused the Earth Consciousness to react violently, sinking the continent into the ocean in just a single day.

Like other great ancient civilizations, Atlantis came to an abrupt and tragic end. But once again, some inhabitants escaped, this time in airships, and traveled to Africa, Spain, and the Andes mountains of South America, where they planted new seeds of civilization.

9. The Transitions of Modern Civilization

After the destruction of Atlantis, surviving citizens were scattered all across the globe. Amon II, who had fled to Egypt, taught people to worship the light and was himself worshipped as a deity. He gave the farmers of Egypt the wisdom and knowledge cultivated in Atlantis. The pyramids that would make the Egyptian civilization so famous were modeled after Amon-Ra's personal pyramid, which he used for worship. Many descendants of refugees from both Mu and Atlantis had gathered in South America, where they had been creating their own unique civilization. These people believed that beings from outer space were gods, and had developed a culture based on communicating with beings from other planets. High up in the mountains of the Andes, they built enormous landing sites for spacecraft.

Then, about seven thousand years ago, a spirit who would become king of the ancient Incan Empire of the Andes incarnated on Earth and took on the name Rient Arl Croud. He declared to his people that beings from outer space were not gods. He taught the mystical teaching that God is not found somewhere outside of us, but within our own hearts. The true purpose of life, he said, is to explore the mysteries of the world within our minds. He taught everyone to strive for higher spiritual states of mind and to seek to become ever closer to God.

Rient Arl Croud was a reincarnation of La Mu from the Mu civilization and of Thoth from Atlantis. This same life force would be born again later as Gautama Siddhartha, also known as Shakyamuni Buddha, who would teach Buddha's Truths in India. (Unlike the souls of the fourth or fifth dimensions, those of the ninth dimension, including Shakyamuni and Jesus, are massive bodies of light energy. Therefore, it's more accurate to say that a portion of the same life force will be born onto Earth than to say that the same soul will reincarnate.)

A little more than four thousand years ago, the soul who would later reincarnate as Jesus was born in Egypt, where he was known as Clario. His teachings were a combination of faith in love and faith in the sun.

Between 3,800 and 3,700 years ago, Zeus was born in Greece. He would later be known as "the omniscient and omnipotent" because of his excellence in both learning and the arts. Since Zeus is the ninth-dimensional spirit in charge of the arts, it's not difficult to see why the culture that Zeus established in Greece was full of beauty. He was wary of the tendency of religions to make people suffer from a sense of guilt, and instead focused his efforts on encouraging his people to cultivate and express their characters in a positive, creative, and free manner. That is why so many of the gods of Greek mythology are so joyful and colorful.

Then, between 3,300 and 3,200 years ago, Moses was born in Egypt, the son of a slave. As an infant, he was set adrift on the Nile in a raft of reeds, but was rescued by Pharaoh's daughter and raised in the royal palace. When he reached adulthood, Moses discovered that he was born of Hebrew parents and eventually led hundreds of thousands of his people on the Exodus from Egypt, across the Red Sea, to Canaan. During his life, he received various revelations from God, such as the famous Ten Commandments.

Some two thousand years ago, Jesus Christ was born among the people of Israel, the descendants of the Hebrews who fled with Moses. Jesus spread the teachings of love among his followers. He was eventually crucified, but was resurrected from the dead, appeared once more before his disciples, and ate with them. His resurrection was actually the materialization of his spirit body, not the revival of his flesh—a fact that is supported by his ascent to Heaven afterwards.

Jesus received guidance from many spirits in Heaven. Among them was Hermes, a Grand Tathagata of love and faith who guided Jesus through the complexities of the resurrection. Christianity spread throughout the world to become a great religion because Jesus dispensed with the worship of the Hebrew god of vengeance (Yahweh) and chose to believe in the God of love (El Cantare). It was the god of vengeance who would cause Jesus to become crucified, but Hermes and other Greek gods worked to elevate Jesus's status from that of a mere prophet to Christ the Savior, and to spread his teachings throughout the Roman Empire and Europe.

In the East, Shakyamuni Buddha taught Buddhism in India 2,500 years ago, and in China, Confucius would spread Confucianism. This is how the seeds of the Laws have been planted throughout the world and have formed and shaped the civilization we live in today.

10. Toward the Golden Age

In this historical survey of the rise and fall of many civilizations of the last million years, we can see five things that all of them had in common.

1. Each civilization had a rise and fall.

2. God, also known as Buddha, provided every civilization with Great Guiding Spirits of Light.

3. When each civilization reached its peak, evil had also risen to great heights. Ominous clouds of dark thought-energy had formed and were casting their shadow over humankind. This led to massive catastrophes, such as the shifting of the Earth's axis or the sinking of whole continents.

4. The wisdom and traditions of older civilizations were passed on as new ones began, but new civilizations also formed their own new sets of values.

5. Every one of these civilizations offered a place for humankind to undergo soul training, and thereby served a necessary and integral role in the process of reincarnation.

The civilization in which we have been living since the latter half of the twentieth century closely resembles Mu and Atlantis in their final years. There is a strong emphasis on science and technology today, causing materialism to spread throughout the world. People's hearts are becoming wayward, social evils are rampant, and many spiritual leaders delude their followers. On the other hand, there are religious leaders throughout the world who are preaching the Truths.

Still, it is not difficult to foresee the future if we look at the fate of past civilizations and compare it to the current state of our own. Given the global nature of the modern world, the disasters that await us will not be limited to just a single continent or civilization; they will be worldwide. Moreover, it is quite possible that they will occur within the next several decades. It is easy for me to make this prophesy because I have the ability to foresee the fate of humankind and to tell you exactly what disasters and catastrophes are awaiting us. However, there is one thing I would like to add. No matter how terrible the catastrophes that befall the world, they do *not* signal the end. In the civilizations of the past, people believed that the disasters they saw meant the end of times. However, seeds of these civilizations survived to establish a new garden of hope, which eventually developed into a civilization of prosperity and light.

The cycles of reincarnation apply not only to human souls, but to entire civilizations and cultures as well. The civilizations of our planet move in continuous cycles from birth to death. Please always keep this thought in your heart: "The end of one thing is always the beginning of another."

I am recording the words of this book, *The Laws of the Sun*, as I receive them from the Cosmic World of the ninth dimension, knowing that Earth is about to plunge into darkness. The world needs a beacon of light to guide it through the coming darkness. Humankind needs the light of Buddha's

Truths to be shining from at least one corner of the world. This book, *The Laws of the Sun*, is part of the majestic sun of Buddha's Truths that is now rising above the horizon. Its light will serve the new civilization that is waiting to arise.

Humankind will brave decades of chaos and destruction as this new millennium unfolds. After these birth pangs, a new civilization will begin in Asia. It will spread from Japan to the countries of Southeast Asia, to Indonesia, and eventually to Oceania. Some continents will sink into the ocean, and the continent of Mu will appear again in the Pacific, becoming the center of a new massive civilization.

Eventually, parts of Europe and North America will also sink beneath the ocean. However, Atlantis will eventually resurface and become an even larger continent than it was before. In the year 2400, Jesus Christ will be reborn on this new continent. Then, in 2800, Moses will incarnate and create a new cosmic civilization on the continent of Garna, which by that time will have reappeared in the Indian Ocean.

Some of you who read this book will reincarnate on Earth during the next coming of Jesus and Moses, and will learn their teachings. However, the welfare of these civilizations depends on whether we who are alive today will be able to help the sun of Buddha's Truths rise all over the world. When the world sinks into darkness, we must become the sun that will shine brilliantly enough to give the world light and hope. In this sense, those who have been born in this age have an important mission.

Fortunately, many of those who helped spread Buddha's Truths in the time of La Mu, Agasha, Shakyamuni Buddha, and Jesus Christ have been reborn in the present era, and among my readers there are numerous bodhisattvas—angels—who will step forward to help.

· 6 ·

THE PATH TO
EL CANTARE

1. *Open Your Eyes*

In chapter 5, we looked back over the history of the last million years. We saw how continents rose from the oceans and returned to them as various civilizations flowered and perished. Do you think the people of these lost civilizations are completely unrelated to you? Quite the contrary. *You* were born in these eras and lived in these civilizations. *You* were the people of Atlantis and the people of Mu. Deep within your soul is a reservoir of memories, a complete record of your past lives in tens or even hundreds of civilizations. Everyone retains these memories. You have a storehouse of the spiritual wisdom that you have acquired through countless reincarnations. Although these memories are imprinted on your soul, you leave your awareness of these memories behind when you are born into this physical world.

Contrary to what you might believe, your physical body is not your true self. I encourage you to awaken to your true self, the soul that animates your body. Your body is like a full-body suit that you need to wear to be born into this world; it is simply a vehicle. Like a ship or a car, your body transports your soul as it undergoes spiritual training in this world. You are the captain of the ship, or the driver of the car, but you are not the ship or the car itself. I would like you to discover the real you.

If you believe that the knowledge you have acquired in this lifetime is the full truth of the world, you are terribly mistaken. Nor can anyone else discover who you really are; you need to seek the truth on your own. To find it, you need to look deep within your mind and explore it thoroughly. Enlightenment is to discover your true self. It gives you the power to say, with confidence, "This is who I am."

The truth is that human souls were originally part of Buddha that then split off from Him. We are works of art that He created to express Himself. Humans are granted the freedom to act and create, but unfortunately, many of us misuse these gifts and live in a selfish and egotistical way, like the Monkey King depicted in the classic Chinese novel *Journey to the West*. Living solely to satisfy our selfish desires and enjoy our earthly lives, we human beings forgot the parent of our souls and neglected His Will. As soon as we became more attached to this material world than to Heaven, we degraded the human race as a whole and created Hell, a world that mirrors the desire and strife we created on Earth.

To know yourself is to know that you are a child of Buddha and to know His Will. To open your eyes is to awaken to your own spirituality and to open your heart to the existence of the spirit world in the fourth dimension and above. Of course, you can choose to keep your eyes closed if you are content with your present self. If you are satisfied with your own life and with the current state of humanity, by all means settle back and enjoy life as you know it. If, however, you want to open your eyes in the truest sense, you must start by exploring the depths of your mind, for there you will find the keys that will lead you to the land of Buddha.

2. Abandon Your Attachments

To know your true self, you must first become aware that you have a false self. This realization is the first step in the process of casting that spurious self aside. The false self has four primary characteristics:

THE SELF THAT TAKES LOVE FROM OTHERS

The first characteristic of the false self is that it thinks only of taking love from others. The Primordial Buddha gave us the universe. He gave us our souls and physical bodies. He gave us everything, including the sun, the air, water, the land, the seas, animals, plants, and minerals, yet He asks for nothing in return. We human beings live in a world where everything we could possibly need is provided, yet all we can think of is how to get more.

How could we even think about receiving more love when we are given all the love we need? Those who are busy taking love from others are simply unaware of His love. So what exactly is this love they want from others? The love they want is to be looked up to by other people. What is the point of such recognition in this world? What good does it do you to be highly respected based on three-dimensional materialistic values? What use is it to anyone? It certainly does nothing to improve our souls. In fact, this kind of admiration only creates barriers between you and others. If we continue on this path, the whole world will resemble a zoo, with all the people in it trapped inside cages of their own making. Those who do not see this truth are clinging to false values. As long as they stay the way they are, they will never be able to attain true happiness.

THE SELF THAT DOES NOT BELIEVE
IN BUDDHA

We should feel most sorry for those who do not have faith in Buddha, who do not believe in the world that He created. For them, humans are born simply as a result of copulation, and every individual life is totally independent of the rest of humankind. This is the most tragic false self. Those who do not believe in Him and insist on seeing proof of His existence mistakenly believe that they can sit in judgment over Him. They have become so arrogant that they believe that they are superior to Him.

But of course, human beings cannot prove the existence of Buddha, who has been guiding humankind since before the Creation of Earth. The only way to obtain that sort of proof would be to die and return to the other world. But people who die without believing in the afterlife will find themselves so confused that even then, they will be unable to recognize their own existence.

THE SELF THAT MAKES NO EFFORTS FOR
SPIRITUAL PROGRESS

The third characteristic of the false self is lacking in efforts for spiritual progress. The false self gives in to laziness, neglects the study of Buddha's Truths, passes unfair judgment on others, and becomes hardheaded. Buddha expects more of us; He asks humans to make an eternal effort, so as His children we must do so.

Do you make a sincere effort every day to deepen your knowledge of the Truths? Do you evaluate the ability and potential of others accurately? Are you open-minded? You won't be able to improve your soul, and therefore won't achieve spiritual progress, if you are closed-minded. Being open-minded is a virtue, and it is what Buddha expects of us. If you are always contradicting others and not listening to what they have to say, you are not open-minded.

THE SELF THAT IS FULL OF WORLDLY ATTACHMENTS

The fourth characteristic of the false self is that it clings to this world. To know your true self is to live every day with His Will as your own, knowing that you are born into this world temporarily to train your soul, and being aware that eventually you must leave everything behind and return to the other world. No matter how much you may wish to remain in this world, one day you will have to depart for the next.

Your life on Earth is impermanent, which is why you must live each day as if it were your last. We never know when we will die. No one in Heaven is attached to the material things of this world, whereas all the inhabitants of Hell remain obsessed with this world. Never forget this, even for a moment.

3. Be Passionate Like a Roaring Fire

Making a resolution to abandon all worldly attachments is one of the biggest decisions you can make in life. It's a decision that requires courage, but it will guarantee happiness for your eternal life. Contrary to what many people may think, this decision does not mean that you have to lead a passive life. In fact, only when you can cut yourself off from your attachments will you be free to live a positive and bold life here on Earth.

Take a look around at other people, and you will see how they weaken themselves by becoming attached to this world. Why do they cling so tightly to their status or reputation? Why are they always comparing their income to that of others? Why are they so proud of their education, or of the corporation for which they work? Why are they forever worrying about what they look like or what other people think about them? What good does it do them to win the admiration of other people? Seen through the eyes of the Creator of the great universe, human attachments are inexpressibly futile and insignificant. I truly hope you appreciate this.

Cast away all earthly desires and become passionate about polishing your mind during your life on Earth. This is how you can live a life of Truth, as a child of Buddha. This is what He expects of us. You cannot take status, reputation, or wealth accumulated on Earth with you when you die and return to the other world. Nor would these things have any meaning there.

Do you know that many people once lauded for their achievements are now suffering in Hell? For example, hundreds of thousands of executives who climbed to enviable positions on Earth are now in the Hell of Lust, the Hell of Strife, and the Hell of Beasts. Those who thought of nothing but making money or who lived solely to satisfy physical desires such as lust now have to suffer for hundreds of years for their limited years of enjoyment on Earth. Hell is not just a myth we tell to scare children. It exists, and it exists at this very moment. Those who have awakened to the Truths can see those souls suffering in Hell as clearly as goldfish in a fish tank. The more attached and obsessed they become on Earth, the deeper their suffering will be in the next world.

Human beings are essentially souls. When we die, the only thing we bring with us to the other world is our mind, the core of our soul. Only when we realize that the mind is all that remains can we change ourselves and take our lives more seriously. If all we take with us is the mind, then we want to make the mind as beautiful as possible. What is a beautiful mind? It is a mind filled with love, a mind that can receive blessings from Buddha. It is, in other words, a mind characterized by giving, nurturing, forgiveness, and gratitude. You must be endlessly passionate about bringing your mind to this glorious state by raising the level of your thoughts.

What, then, is the opposite of worldly attachment? Love. This is because love is based on giving. To truly love others is to let go of your impulse to cling to them, and to keep loving them without expecting anything in return. Giving love is where you must begin.

What have you done for your parents, who raised and took care of you? What have you done for your brothers and sisters? Have you lived up to the expectations of your teachers? What have you done for your friends? What have you done for your girlfriend or boyfriend, your wife or your husband? What have you done for the people whose paths have crossed your own during your lifetime? As you raised your children, did you consider the sacrifices your own parents made when they were raising you? Have you forgiven anyone you once hated or resented? Have you let go of your anger towards others? How much have you been able to respond to Buddha's love, and as a result, how brave have you become in walking your path through life?

4. *Life Is a Succession of Daily Challenges*

After you commit to letting go of your worldly attachments, purifying your heart, and living as a child of Buddha, what's the next step? It is not to live like a hermit in the mountains, become an ascetic, or spend most of your time sitting in meditation. We're not born on Earth to live in isolation, any more than we're born to give up eating. Two thousand five hundred years ago, Shakyamuni Buddha showed us that enlightenment could not be achieved in these ways, and the example of his life should be sufficient to establish that the seeds of enlightenment are not to be found in physical sacrifice alone. Nor are the seeds of enlightenment to be found in a life devoted to sensual pleasures. What Buddha expects of us is that we abandon both extremes and lead a life of the Middle Way of these. We human beings are essentially souls, or minds, but this doesn't mean that we should neglect our physical bodies. Your body, after all, is a valuable gift from Him, given to you as the vehicle for your spiritual learning in this world. Some people love their cars so much that they religiously wash and wax them. Think how much more care we should take of our bodies!

To stay healthy, we need to exercise, eat a balanced diet, make sure we get enough sleep, and live a well-regulated life. We should not lose our souls to alcohol or to other substances that can distort our perceptions. Once people become addicted, they can no longer think rationally, which allows the devils of Hell to possess and control their bodies. As a result, they become tormented, often failing in the workplace and wreaking havoc in their families.

It's easy to say that we should avoid extremes and take the Middle Way, but it is very difficult to actually live this way. The more thought we put into taking the Middle Way, the more we realize how profound it is. You may well ask, "What principles can we follow to make sure that we are taking the Middle Way?" There are two basic guidelines you can follow. One is to reflect on your life based on the Eightfold Path. The other is to see your life in terms of the developmental stages of love.

The Eightfold Path, as I have mentioned, teaches Right View, Right Thought, Right Speech, Right Action, Right Livelihood, Right Effort, Right Mindfulness, and Right Concentration. It provides a method for preventing your thoughts and actions from swinging to extremes, which helps you to find the Middle Way, a path to a life of peace and harmony. But if you limit yourself to a life of reflection, you will find it difficult to progress any further. Once you've considered your thoughts and deeds and realized where you have gone wrong, what is your next step? You will feel gratitude, which will make you want to take action. What can you do to express gratitude? Is it saying "thank you" to others? Of course that's one way, but I suggest you take a more proactive approach: love others. The truest expression of gratitude is to never stop giving; gratitude is the practice of giving love without expecting anything in return.

From time to time, take a look at yourself and consider which stage of love you have reached: fundamental love, spiritually nurturing love, forgiving love, or love incarnate. The stages of love provide you with a way to measure your spiritual progress and gauge your development day by day. When your life is based on the guidelines of self-reflection and progress, you are truly living as a child of Buddha. Practice self-reflection every day: check to see if you had extreme thoughts or actions, and based on the developmental stages of love, look within yourself to see what progress you have made. Only by doing this will you truly be able to overcome the challenges of everyday life and live according to the Middle Way.

5. When Our Souls Sparkle

While we need to reflect and make progress based on our findings, these alone do not add beauty to our life or bring a sparkle to our souls. I believe that there are three moments in life that bring us this luster, these brilliant sparks of animation. The first occurs when we recover from illness. Illness is a trial that can bring us physical and mental suffering, and the way we battle illness shows what kind of people we really are. Illness is commonly caused by an irregular lifestyle, overwork, or destructive thoughts, which means that when you suffer from a physical illness, you have problems in your mind as well. So when you become sick, search your mind for reasons for your physical suffering.

Almost 80 percent of all human illness is caused by spiritual possession. Spirits who cannot return to Heaven often possess people and inflict on them the same kind of suffering and pain that these spirits experienced while they were alive. There are many instances in which, as soon as the spirit is removed from a seriously ill patient, the sick person's fever goes down and he or she feels refreshed in body and mind and starts walking around freely without any pain. This shows how susceptible the human body is to spiritual influences.

Possessing spirits hate it when people repent for their wrong thoughts and deeds and begin to feel gratitude. Because when sick people repent and feel gratitude, their auras begin to shine and their spiritual vibrations change. Now the spirits have no choice but to leave them. To let this aura shine even more brightly, look closely at the things you cling to, and let go of these attachments one by one. Ironically, when sick people have no regrets in this world, at the point when they are ready to die, they will receive the light of Truth from Heaven, assisted by their guardian spirits and Guiding Spirits, and experience a rapid recovery from the illness. This is truly a miraculous moment. After a dramatic shift like this, people start living as if they had been reborn. The light they experience not only changes their lives, but also shines into the hearts of others.

The second sparkling moment of life takes place when we awaken to faith. Living without faith is like groping through the dark, whereas living with faith gives us a bright lantern to light the way. When you are blinded by materialistic values, you become too enamored of physical pleasures and become interested only in competition; you forget that Buddha is watching over you. This is the greatest tragedy. It is only through the luminous power of faith that human beings who remain closed to the existence of the spirit world can open their eyes to the Truths.

The third moment that our soul sparkles takes place when we receive revelations, or spiritual messages from Heaven, when our mind opens and we are able to communicate directly with our guardian spirits or Guiding Spirits. This is very different from the dangerous psychic or supernatural phenomena caused by sennin spirits, which are often just performances meant to amuse or to show off the psychic person's metaphysical powers.* The words these spirits speak do not

---

* Sennin spirits reside in the back side of Heaven (in the Sennin Realm). Their main goal is to perfect their supernatural powers, and sennins tend to lack human warmth and kindness. (Refer to *The Nine Dimensions*. IRH Press, 2012)

contain teachings of the Truths. When people get absorbed in these supernatural phenomena, they start speaking nonsense and often end up suffering mental breakdowns. The spiritual messages we receive at Happy Science come from Divine Spirits who share their enlightened wisdom, and only those with a high level of enlightenment can receive them. These spiritual messages serve as proof that we are not only guided by these Divine Spirits but are also protected by them. Whether you receive these messages directly from the Divine Spirits or learn them through books or videos, this wonderful experience is the third type of sparkling moment in life.

6. Time that Shines Like the Diamond

To live your life boldly, you must make full use of your limited time on Earth. Human souls are given the opportunity to be reborn on Earth once every few hundred years—sometimes only once every few thousand years—so it is a very precious experience. However, the vast majority of people never give any serious thought to why they are alive. Some awaken to faith toward the end of their lives and pledge to make a new start. But they cannot go back and start over again. Time is like an arrow, or like water in a river: once it passes, it will not return. This is not to say that those who awaken to the Truths later in life won't live a meaningful life.

If they're determined to live the remainder of their days based on the Truths, they will enjoy a valuable and fruitful life. But blessed are those who awaken to Buddha's Truths in their youth, for they can live to the fullest.

The secret to living a meaningful life is to meditate on the moment of your death. What thoughts will you have? How will you feel about the way you've spent your life? Would you be proud of the way you've lived? Would you have any regrets? Have you lived in good conscience? Take some time to consider these questions. Good thoughts and feelings mean that your life has been filled with happiness. But regrets indicate that you are more likely to feel remorse for your mistakes when you stand in front of the Divine Spirits in the other world; there, your entire life will be shown on a screen and watched by a large audience of spirits.

This is how people who return to the spirit world in the fourth dimension realize what kind of person they are in the eyes of Buddha. At that time, there will be no room for lies or excuses. People destined for Hell will choose to go there themselves because they feel too ashamed to live in Heaven. According to the physics of the spirit world, such people's coarse and agitated spiritual vibrations prevent them from staying in a realm inhabited by spirits with refined and serene spiritual vibrations. Their consciousness has taken on so many of this world's materialistic values that their spiritual bodies have become heavy, and naturally sink.

There are also people who will receive applause when their life story is shown in the spirit world. After a scene in which they find faith, realize the mistakes they have made, and ask Buddha for His forgiveness with tears in their eyes, the audience will congratulate and embrace these newcomers. When the "film" comes to a moment in which they determine to devote their lives to spreading Buddha's Truths, bodhisattvas of light will rejoice with tears of delight.

Sooner or later, you will face death, and then your life too will be reviewed in the other world. This is why I encourage you to keep the last moments of your life in mind and to keep asking yourself if you are living in a way that will leave you with no regret. This is what I mean by living every day as if it were the last day of your life. Anticipate your biography being screened in the other world, and consider how it would look from the audience's perspective to see everything you have ever done and have ever thought of doing. This is the secret to making your life shine like a diamond, to living a meaningful and fruitful life that sparkles like this most precious of jewels.

7. Embrace Your Dreams

Everyone needs a dream. A life without dreams is a life without hope. Of course it's important to realize your mistakes, repent, and restore a good heart, but doing this only brings you up from a deficit state to zero. At the end of your life, if you end up where you started from, you haven't made the most of the challenge.

To embrace a dream, you need to make the best possible plan for your life. If you were to build a house, you would hire an architect to create a blueprint and contractors to construct your home based on the architect's design. The architect of your life is none other than you. To build a good house, you need a proper plan and a careful design. You should put at least as much thought and work into structuring your own life. Too many people live without concrete plans, just taking everything as it comes.

Making a plan for your life is not as difficult as you may think. Just embrace a dream and visualize how you'll make it come true. People with dreams have confidence in the lives they live and are convincing when they talk about their future. When you meet them, you not only want to help them; you also become inspired to take on new challenges yourself.

There is something about embracing a dream that intoxicates people. I'm sure everyone throughout history who accomplished remarkable things for the benefit of future generations started with a dream. Having the rare good fortune to be born in this world as a human being, it's extremely important to try to accomplish something great. Don't let modesty keep you from thinking big. Modesty is only necessary when you become overconfident. In other words, modesty acts as a kind of brake to keep your car from careening out of control, but you can't drive a car with just a brake pedal. To fulfill its intended purpose, it also needs an accelerator.

On numerous occasions I have warned of the danger of falling into Hell, but I don't want you to spend too much time worrying about it. If you devote all your time to praying and chanting sutras to avoid Hell, you'll never achieve any growth. Once you set the course of your life in the right direction, put your foot down on the accelerator and only use the brake when you're going too fast. If you realize you've made a mistake, reflect on it and change direction. So long as you know the brake will work when you need it, travel full speed toward your dream. That is how you'll make it come true.

Guiding your life plan is not the only benefit of having a dream. With a dream—a vision that you keep in your mind—comes mystical power. This vision becomes known to your guardian spirit and Guiding Spirits in the other world, who are always looking for ways to protect and guide people on Earth. But these spirits can't guide our every move, because that would deprive us of independence and free will; all they can do is provide inspiration. The fact that most people on Earth have only fleeting thoughts about their lives and no concrete plan makes it very difficult for spirits to guide them.

However, if you do have a clear dream, your guardian spirit and Guiding Spirits can do more than just encourage you; they can help you come up with ways to achieve it.

This is how you can achieve true self-realization. First, embrace a dream. (It goes without saying that your dream should lead to the improvement of your soul and to the happiness of other people.) Then, visualize your dream and pray to your guardian spirit and Guiding Spirits for guidance. In due time, your dream will become reality.

8. The Golden Ax of Courage

Courage. The very sound of the word makes my heart leap, and I don't believe I'm the only one who feels this way. When I hear the word *courage*, I can almost hear the steady strokes of a woodsman in the forest like the pulse of life. Human beings are all given an ax called courage, and with this ax, we can cut our way through the giant trees of adversity that block our path. When you feel weighed down by the pressures of life, when you feel miserable and full of despair, remember that Buddha has given you the ax of courage.

We are born on Earth spiritually blindfolded. We have to rely on our five senses to guide us through the darkness. That is why He has endowed each of us with the ax of courage hanging from our belt, but all too often we don't think of using it. When you face trouble and sadness, instead of looking to others for solutions or asking for their pity, reach for the ax of courage and cut the ropes of fate that bind you.

A highly enlightened Chinese Zen master, Wumen Huikai (1183–1260) wrote a collection of forty-eight koans in a book entitled *The Gateless Gate*.* This is an excerpt from "The Enlightened Man," his twentieth koan.

The priest Shōgen asked, "Why does the enlightened man not stand on his feet and explain himself?" Then he added, "It is not necessary for speech to come from the tongue."

Wumen's commentary:
Shōgen spoke plainly enough, but how many will understand him? Anyone who comprehends his meaning should come to my place, and I will test out my Zen stick on him. Why? Because to test real gold, you must see it in fire.

Wumen's verse:
If the feet of the enlightened man moved,
The great ocean would overflow;

---

* A koan is a question, dialogue, story, or statement used in Zen practice to contemplate and deepen one's enlightenment. Each koan in *The Gateless Gate* is accompanied by a commentary and verse by Wumen.

If that head bowed,
It would look down upon the heavens.
Such a body has no place to rest . . .
Please finish this verse with your own words.

This koan tells us that we human beings have forgotten the immense power we carry within us. We have been hypnotized by commonly accepted beliefs, by what others have taught us; we believe that we are nothing more than this physical body that could break down any moment. Yet we are truly children of Buddha, and as such, we have infinite power. If you meditate and reach spiritual liberation, you will become aware of your real spiritual nature, like a giant looking down on Earth. You will see that from the perspective of the multidimensional universe, our three-dimensional galaxy, like the "great ocean" of the koan, is no more than a puddle beneath your feet. The worlds of human enlightenment, below the sixth dimension, are located so far below your true self that you need to tilt your head to see them.

Wumen Huikai's awareness reached the World of Tathagatas (the eighth dimension) while he was still alive. When you attain this level of enlightenment, you realize that human beings are not just individual souls in physical bodies, but large energy-bodies extending far out into the universe. In meditation, you will experience your spiritual energy expanding until you can look down upon the Earth far below.

Human beings are endowed with complete freedom and infinite potential, but we bind ourselves with reliance on our physical senses and with conventional knowledge and schooling. To deny the existence of the spirit world or the soul is to limit yourself. If you are unaware of your true nature, when you fall ill, you may see yourself as a miserable tiny being and be assailed by the fear of death.

Take heart; boldly and steadily swing the golden ax of courage, and fell the giant tree of delusion. Conquer your worries and suffering, and slash yourself free from the shackles of fate.

Courage is invaluable. When you use it to realize your innate power, you will rise from your sickbed and begin a vigorous life. You will awaken to the Truths and dispel the delusions of materialism. But even then, since you're still living in the three-dimensional world, you may find yourself giving in to temptations and starting to lose enthusiasm. But this is the very moment when you must fight off the urge to give up. When you run in a marathon, you reach a point when you feel so exhausted that you want to drop out, but if you fight through it, the pain passes, your feet feel lighter, and you make it to the finish line. The same is true for swimming. When you swim in a long-distance race, there comes a time when your whole body seems to cry out for you to stop, but if you keep going, you will feel your body become one with the water, and you are able to continue. If you had given up, you would never have been able to reach the finish line, let alone win the race.

Of course, life is not exactly the same as running a marathon or swimming long distances, but the point is that in any endeavor, we will face moments of trial. It is by enduring and overcoming these hard times that we gain confidence and feel the closeness of Buddha's love and mercy.

9. Memories of My Early Days

My own life serves as an example of this principle of making continuous and diligent effort to overcome adversity and to open up a path. In my last years of elementary school, I was able to put in particularly long hours of study for a student my age. As a result, I was able to achieve an average test score of 99.7 percent in my sixth year at the school.

With my report card in his hand, my father went to discuss my future with his acquaintance, the headmaster of a junior high school affiliated with a famous university. He told my father that I would have no problem qualifying for his school. In fact, he said that with my grades, I would be easily accepted to Nada Junior High, one of the best junior high schools in the country. But my father thought that it would be better for me to stay in my hometown in case I wanted to pursue a career in politics.

I passed the entrance exam with a perfect score and entered Kawashima Junior High School in my hometown. My junior high school days were filled with happy memories: I served as the head of the student union, the captain of the tennis team, and the editor and publisher of the school newspaper. All these experiences helped shape my leadership skills. My success in academic studies continued. I managed to place first in national examinations on several occasions, astonishing the teachers. It seems just yesterday that my homeroom teacher came to me in my third year and told me that it was unusual for a top student to be genuinely popular with his peers, as I was. She went on to say, "For some reason, everyone listens to you, and no one ever disagrees with what you have to say." I realize now that I already possessed the qualities necessary to become a religious leader.

When it was time to go on to high school, I decided to apply to the Tokushima Jōnan High School, the best school in my prefecture. At the time, there was pressure to prevent students in rural areas from attending high school in the cities so that they would stay in their hometowns. A new entrance examination scheme based on the Tokyo model had been put into place. This system permitted the top 10 percent of students to attend the school of their choice, while the remaining 90 percent had to go to local schools allocated by lottery. Not wanting my future to be left to chance, I studied hard, became the top student in my area, and in due course entered Tokushima Jōnan High School. This school had an excellent record of placing students at the University of Tokyo, the best university in the country, so I started to consider going there myself.

Unfortunately, my time in high school was nothing like my happy days in junior high. I was often feeling exhausted from the grueling kendo practices* and the two-and-a-half-hour commute between school and home. Because I needed all the time I could find for my studies, I did nearly all my English studies by the dim light of a noisy train. I would stand in the swaying carriage with an English textbook in my right hand, a dictionary in my left, and a fountain pen between my fingers, struggling to answer questions. My face must have revealed how intensely I was concentrating, because one time, a little girl about four years old stood up and offered me her seat!

Although I never felt I had enough time to study, I managed to come in at the top of my class. My favorite subject was Japanese, and in my first year of high school I got top marks in a national distance-learning course six times in a row, which gave me a lot of self-confidence. (As far as I know,

---

* Kendo is a Japanese form of fencing based on traditional swordsmanship, usually played with two-handed bamboo swords.

this record still stands today.) Perhaps it wasn't such a good idea to devote so much time to the art of language, since it didn't help me get into college, but it did become very helpful in later years, when I began to read and write many books and give talks to large audiences.

Other subjects I enjoyed were geography and biology, although they, too, weren't tested in the university entrance exam. I excelled in liberal arts, especially English, Japanese, and social studies, but in my second year I decided to take science courses that required me to take more mathematics and physics classes. This led some people to believe that I was interested in applying to the medical program at the University of Tokyo, but I had already decided to apply to the law school there because it would provide me with a wider range of possibilities for my future.

In my first and second years of high school, I played the lead role in the school play. Although I felt that I was the wrong person for it, perhaps I had a talent that I was unaware of, because a member of the drama club repeatedly asked me to join. Later, when I started talking in front of large audiences, I wished that I had joined the drama club and gained more stage experience, but by then, of course, it was too late.

During my final year in high school, I went back to liberal arts courses. The level of these courses was very high. Five of the liberal arts students in my year eventually entered the law program at the University of Tokyo, and one entered the economics program. I was not entirely satisfied with my own academic achievements, but I graduated from high school with an award for best students.

Before taking my university entrance exam, I tried a practice test and was relieved when my results predicted that I would pass the exam and place within the top tenth percentile. I scored even higher in the real exam, and in the spring of 1976, I entered the law program at the University of Tokyo. At that time in Japan, those who studied law at the University of Tokyo had the reputation of being the country's best and the brightest, and I became worried that I might not be able to keep up. Feeling desperately in need of extra study, I immersed myself in a variety of subjects day and night: I studied not only law and politics, but also social studies, history, philosophy, economics, management, natural sciences, and international relations. I read books in English and German, and was surprised to find that I could read English much faster than the university lecturers and professors. I remember once turning up at my favorite local coffee shop with a thick English book on European political history. I became so involved in reading that when I looked up, I saw that the owner was telling new customers that the coffee shop was closed so that he could provide me with a quiet space to read.

But I didn't spend all my time studying. On sunny days, I used to walk around Hanegi park in the late afternoon and stroll through the town of Umegaoka, and I would jot down verses of poetry that came to me as I walked. I would look at the sky at sunset and ponder Plato's thoughts on the spirit world or Kitarō Nishida's ideas of "pure experience" and "self-awareness." I was awakening spiritually in those days, unconsciously preparing for my future role as a religious leader.

When my happy days at the liberal arts campus in Komaba came to an end, I moved on to the school of law at Hongo Campus. My grades remained very high, and my most memorable accomplishment at the time was probably the research paper I wrote during the spring vacation of my third year, entitled "The World of Hannah Arendt's Values." Arendt was an American political philosopher who was strongly influenced by ancient Greek political thought. I read all her works, which are written in Germanic English and are famous for their intricacy. For two weeks, I stayed up every night working on my paper until six in the morning. My friends remarked that my paper was too difficult to understand, but my professor praised it as a mature work, and said it showed promise of a successful career in academics. If it were to be expanded, he said, and given a proper introduction, it might even be suitable for submission as a doctoral thesis. At the same time that he offered this praise, my professor expressed concern that I was so deeply involved in philosophy, which might mean that I was not cut out for the pragmatism of law.

I was twenty-one years old then, and starting to show signs of academic genius, yet I had a tendency to take lightly practical subjects such as constitutional law, civil law, and criminal law, preferring more abstract metaphysical subjects. My law professor had high expectations for me, and he stressed that, as a law student, it was imperative that I study subjects that had practical applications in society. In response, I joined the mass of students in the Hongo library who were studying the Japanese Compendium of Laws and all the cases and precedents that it comprises.

But I remained unconvinced that law was a genuinely academic subject of study. For example, I could not stop thinking about the fundamental intent behind the implementation of the Japanese Constitution, and I felt sorry for those of my fellow students who devoted themselves to memorizing the entire constitution and various theories based on it for the sole purpose of passing the exam. As for criminal law, I wasn't satisfied with the explanations given in the class about the moral basis for giving some people the right to judge and punish others, or with the definitions of crime and the criteria for judging them that the textbook cited. I also kept wondering about the correlation between civil law and Hegel's *The Philosophy of Right*. Commercial law, including corporate law, was too businesslike and seemed to lack depth, since I was much more interested in the philosophy and ideology behind the law.

I had similar reservations about political science. I was

particularly disappointed by one of the professors whose lecture on the theory of political process didn't make logical sense to me.* I was also disappointed when another professor, who taught international politics, argued against the U.S.-Japan Security Treaty based on his left-wing beliefs. I thought the conclusions he reached were wrong, and my belief was confirmed when the Cold War ended and the Soviet Union collapsed.

When I came face to face with the lack of value logic (axiology) in the law and politics I was being taught, I realized that there was not a single professor in the University of Tokyo that I wished to study under. I felt that I had no alternative but to forge my own path. I would have to accumulate sufficient funds to allow me to survive until I could find an academic subject worth studying, or if there was none, to create a completely new field of my own.

At the beginning of my fourth year, I began my preparations for the bar exam by attending a preparatory school for six months. I got top scores there six times, my practice essays were selected as model answers, and many people who studied my answers passed the bar exams. As for me, although I passed the short-answer part of my exams with flying colors, my essays did not get a passing mark, to the surprise of my

---

* This theory was based on Kunio Yanagita'a work on Japanese native forkloristics and Shichihei Yamamoto's analysis of the Japanese people.

colleagues. I think this was due to the fact that I chose not to write the essays from a practical perspective, but from a scholarly point of view. I pointed out faults in some conventional legal theories and disputed some of the accepted interpretations of case precedents. My answers, which criticized the country's Supreme Court, probably shocked the people who graded the exams.

When I discussed this later with the Divine Spirits, I found that they had been determined to take any measure necessary to prevent me from passing the exam and getting a fulfilling job because that might have kept me from pursuing my destiny as a religious leader. So, as it turned out, I really stood no chance of passing the bar.

Quite unexpectedly, the personnel manager of a large trading firm came to see me and asked me to work for his firm. One of the company's managing directors, a graduate of my university who had obtained an MBA from Stanford University, also invited me to join the company, and eventually, out of respect for him, I agreed to take the job. My friends were very critical of my decision in light of the fact that I had turned down my professor's offer to recommend me for the only opening available at the prestigious Bank of Japan. A personnel manager from a government-affiliated bank also came to see me and suggested that I join his bank. He thought highly of me and said that more than half the students from the University of Tokyo who passed the short-answer part of the bar exam on their first try also passed the entrance exam to the bank—a ratio much higher than any other university in the country. He was quite sure, he said, that having majored in political science, I would pass their entrance exam with top marks.

But I had no intention of looking for a job that would offer me a lifetime of security. I preferred to start from scratch and test my own abilities. My friends, however, were worried that I wouldn't survive in a trading firm. They said, "You don't drink, you don't play mahjong, you're not very good at socializing, and you've never been abroad. You are definitely not cut out for the life of a Japanese businessman." Since I could see that they were genuinely worried about me, I became increasingly unsure about whether I had made the right decision.

As graduation day approached, my love of study continued to grow, and I immersed myself in such books as Carl Hilty's *Happiness* and Martin Heidegger's *Being and Time*. As I read them, I couldn't help but feel a strong desire to become a thinker, and this desire only grew stronger over time. So I spent my days reading philosophy and religion in an effort to find the purpose and meaning of life.

10. *The Way to Enlightenment*

On the afternoon of March 23, 1981, I was sitting in the warm spring sunshine reflecting on my life. I was twenty-four years old, and I knew that it was my destiny to leave my business career and become a thinker around the age of thirty, but it was evident that I would need to become financially independent first. I felt that if I continued my own studies and accumulated social experiences while making a living at the trading firm, a path would open before me.

As I contemplated my plans for the future, I sensed an invisible presence in the room. I somehow knew that this other being wished to communicate with me, so I grabbed a pencil and some blank note cards. Of its own volition, my hand picked up the pencil and began to write the words "Good news, Good news."

"Who are you?" I asked. My hand signed the name "Nikkō" on the card. This was how Nikkō, one of the six senior disciples of the thirteenth-century Buddhist monk Nichiren, first made contact with me.

I was astounded. I had no previous connection to the Nichiren sect of Buddhism. But since "Good news" meant "gospel," I realized that the moment of my spiritual awakening had come. I was particularly astonished to be able to confirm the existence of spiritual beings and to verify that human beings did indeed have eternal life.

Suddenly, a number of strange events that had taken place over the previous few months began to make sense. I had occasionally seen a strange glow in my eyes and a golden aura at the back of my head. Some time earlier, when I was still a student in the liberal arts course, I had paid a visit to a temple complex at Mount Koya, and while walking towards the inner sanctum, I had a vision of using mystical powers in the future. Later the same year, I bought a used book called *Shōsetsu Shinsōkan*, by Masaharu Taniguchi, and one night I tried the meditation he taught in the book. When I put my hands together, I felt a strong spiritual power, like a surge of electricity, between my hands. I was quite startled and never opened the book again. But looking back on these events, I could see that my spiritual eye had been starting to open. I then recalled an even earlier spiritual experience in my final year at elementary school. I was lying in bed with a very high fever when I had several out-of-body experiences. My soul left my body and traveled to the spirit world, where I visited Heaven and various realms of Hell, including the Hell of Agonizing Cries. From an early age I was very intuitive, and sensitive to spiritual matters.

The contact from Nikkō in the form of automatic writing soon came to an end. Thereafter Nichiren, Nikkō's master, started contacting me instead. At the time, I thought

Nichiren had contacted me because I had been a student of the Nichiren sect of Buddhism in my previous life (I later discovered that this was not the case). One of the messages Nichiren sent me during this early communication was "love, nurture, and forgive others." This phrase became the basis of my teaching of the developmental stages of love in later years. For at least a year, Nichiren continued to contact me regularly, perhaps because he wanted my help exposing some of the organizations that propagated false teachings in his name.

11. The Appearance of Christ and the Mission of Buddha

In June 1981, an absolutely extraordinary event took place: the spirit of Jesus Christ spoke through me. Speaking in Japanese with a trace of a foreign accent, he expressed his profound love, passion and sincerity. My father was with me at the time, and he was shocked speechless by the presence of a Divine Spirit from the ninth dimension. When spirits from higher dimensions visit, you are enveloped by a numinous radiance that makes your body become very warm. The messages they convey are so full of Truth and light that you feel overwhelmed and moved to tears.

The following month, July, a hidden part of my subconscious was unlocked, and my past reincarnation as Gautama Siddhartha—Shakyamuni Buddha—began to speak to me passionately in a mixture of Japanese and an ancient Indian language that I intuitively understood. He revealed to me that I was an incarnation of El Cantare, the supreme consciousness of the Shakyamuni Buddha soul group,* and explained that it was my mission to bring salvation to all humankind through worldwide dissemination of the Truths. My role as El Cantare was twofold, he said. One aspect was the role of the Amitabha (the Savior), who represents love, mercy, and faith, and the other is the Mahavairocana (the essence of Buddha), who embodies enlightenment, spiritual discipline, and the secret doctrines of the spirit world. If the first aspect were to become more prominent, I would become a Grand Savior, but if the second facet predominated, I would become the embodiment of the Mahavairocana Buddha, the origin of the Vairocana Buddha described in the Flower Garland Sutra and Mahavairocana Sutra.

I was completely shocked by this. My upbringing had been religious, and since childhood I had accepted without question the existence of the spirit world. But this experi-

* The El Cantare consciousness consists of ninth-dimension souls. The reincarnations of El Cantare are as follows: (1) La Mu (born in Mu), (2) Thoth (born in Atlantis), (3) Rient Arl Croud (born in ancient Incan Empire), (4) Ophealis (born in Greece), (5) Hermes (born in Greece), (6) Gautama Siddhartha (born in India), and (7) Ryuho Okawa (born in Japan).

ence was so overpowering, and my destined mission seemed so enormous, that I could not help but be stunned. But one thing was clear to me: as a reincarnation of Shakyamuni Buddha, it was my mission to reorganize the Divine Spirits in Heaven while also integrating all the various religions on Earth to create a new world religion. It had become my responsibility to bring all the people of the world into this new faith, to teach and guide them to pioneer the development of a new civilization, and thus to herald the advent of a new age.

To undertake this incredible responsibility, however, I felt that I needed more understanding of the workings of the spirit world and also to accumulate more experience in my human life. So I decided to continue working at my job with the trading firm, but only until I reached the age of thirty. Shortly after that decision, my life took a dramatic turn, contrary to what I had in mind. In 1982, I was assigned to my company's New York headquarters. The man who had received direct messages from Jesus Christ and had been notified the mission as a Buddha was going to be working long hours with his colleagues on Wall Street in the intense world of international finance!

After a hundred hours of private English lessons at the Berlitz language school, I was interviewed by a professor at the City University of New York who commented that I had a perfect command of the language. I went on to study international finance in a class of native English speakers. I mingled with young businessmen and women in their early thirties from such companies as the Bank of America, Citibank, and Merrill Lynch, and together we learned the ins and outs of the foreign currency exchange system. But I was less than happy in what I was doing. An unbridgeable gap between the realities of my everyday life and my spiritual experiences was growing wider. Sometimes I would find myself looking up at the World Trade Center in lower Manhattan, where I worked, wondering what was truly real: these huge buildings piercing the sky, or the voices I could hear in my heart. My faith and sense of identity were severely tested.

The year I spent as a trainee was nonetheless a great success, and my boss offered me a full-time position in New York. It was a great opportunity, and a clear signal that I was on my way to the top of the professional tree. But I was more interested in the manuscript I was working on, a compilation of the spiritual messages that I had been receiving. So I turned down the offer and recommended a junior colleague for the position instead. People perceived this as an incredible act of selflessness and generosity, rare in the business world, but I returned to Japan knowing that I had taken a decisive step towards my destiny as a religious leader.

I spent the next two years preparing myself for my true mission. In July 1985, I published *The Spiritual Message of Nichiren,* followed by *The Spiritual Message of Kūkai, The Spiritual Message* of Jesus Christ, *The Spiritual Message of Amaterasu-ōmikami*,* and *The Spiritual Message of Socrates*. I was still working for the trading firm in Japan, so these books were published under my father's name, with my own name appearing only as a collaborator.

A year later, in June 1986, Jesus Christ, Ame-no-minaka-nushi-no-kami, and other spirits came to me and declared that it was time to step into my role as a religious leader. On July 15 of that year—a week after my thirtieth birthday—I handed in my resignation to the company and took my first step on the path to fully embracing my mission.

I started writing the first version of *The Laws of the Sun* toward the end of August, and completed it by the beginning of September. I began to write *The Golden Laws* in October and finished it in about a month. Both of these works, published the following year, attracted widespread attention among people seeking the Truths. The doctrine I laid out in *The Laws of the Sun* would also serve as the foundation of Happy Science, an organization I would establish later on.

---

* Amaterasu-ōmikami is a Shinto goddess who was born about 2,600 years ago in present-day Ōita prefecture in Japan and who became the queen of Takachiho. Since her return to the spirit world, she has been worshipped as a Guiding Spirit of Shintoism.

12. *Believe in Me and Follow Me*

I gave my first public lecture at the Ushigome Public Hall in Tokyo on March 8, 1987. Some four hundred people turned up to hear me speak on "The Principles of Happiness." In that talk, I introduced the four basic principles that constitute the core of what I teach—the principles of love, wisdom, self-reflection, and progress. I also announced my plans for the spiritual movement I had launched. We would dedicate the first three years to studying and constructing the basic teachings of the Truths, training religious lecturers, and establishing management policies. Thereafter, we would concentrate on spreading the Truths as widely as possible, both nationally and worldwide.

In April 1987 we published the first issue of our monthly magazine. Together, the articles featured in this magazine and my public lectures set the direction and course of our movement. I began to offer more seminars and public lectures, and as a result we saw a steady increase in committed members who would later become Happy Science lecturers and staff members.

My impassioned lectures inspired and captured the hearts of people all over Japan, and attendance at my public talks kept increasing. By 1988, Hibiya Public Hall, which was designed to hold two thousand people, could not accommodate all who came. In 1989, the audience completely filled the Ryogoku Kokugikan, an indoor stadium with a capacity of 8,500. In 1990, the exhibition hall at Makuhari, which holds well over ten thousand people, was filled to capacity every time I spoke there.

Four years after my initial lecture, on March 7, 1991, Happy Science was officially established as a religious organization. Our new status gave us more momentum to spread our movement and message to the world. The object of worship was the Grand Tathagata Shakyamuni, who is now called El Cantare, supreme leader of the ninth-dimension Grand Spirits. El Cantare has the highest authority to guide Divine Spirits in Heaven and is now living on Earth as the most revered Buddha.

The first annual public celebration of my birth on Earth took place in Tokyo Dome in July 1991, with no fewer than fifty thousand devoted believers in attendance. This meant that only four months after Happy Science was officially incorporated as a religious organization, it had already become one of the largest religious bodies in Japan. Such miraculous growth has never been achieved by any other religious group. At the celebration, I declared that I was El Cantare and revealed my mission as the Buddha of Salvation.

In September of that year, we started a movement called the "Revolution of Hope," whose aim was to expose the injustices of the Japanese mass media, which was casting a dark cloud over people's minds and producing an atmosphere of spiritual darkness. This represented a turning point in the battle to create an ideal society in postwar Japan. By the time we held our annual celebration, the El Cantare Festival, in December 1991, Happy Science had become the most influential religious organization in Japan, with a membership exceeding 5.6 million. In 1992 and 1993, I realigned the foundation of my teachings with Buddhist principles. My lectures were broadcast simultaneously throughout the country, and as the "Revolution of Hope" campaign attracted followers all over Japan, our membership approached ten million.

In this way, our "Miracle Plan," which took place between 1991 and 1993, marked a tremendous success and contributed to the establishment of Happy Science as a religion with faith in El Cantare. In 1994, our highly anticipated "Big Bang Plan" began to spread our faith all over the world. Today, Happy Science has truly become a world religion, with twelve million members worldwide. We must tell all people of the world about the incarnation of El Cantare and about His mission on Earth. It is the Coming, the Advent, of the supreme Buddha, the greatest Savior on Earth. The world is in the process of undergoing purification. With faith in El Cantare, humanity can achieve its final, highest, and greatest salvation.

Spread this message to people all over the world:

Believe in me and follow me. I am your Eternal Master.

AFTERWORD

—From the 1994 Japanese Edition—

The Laws of the Sun is a singular book. No other book has ever revealed the vast framework of Buddha's Truths, including the genesis of all things and creatures, the stages of love, the structure of enlightenment, and a detailed account of the rise, fall, and movement of civilizations. I have also described the purpose and mission of Happy Science, which is devoted to spreading these Truths. Last but not least, *The Laws of the Sun* unveils the sacred mission of El Cantare. I encourage you to believe what is revealed here, for it will be read by future generations, including yourself in your future lives, as the new Bible and the new Buddhist scripture of humankind.

Some noteworthy revisions have been made from the older edition. While the original edition explained the spirit world simply as a dichotomy between Heaven and Hell, this edition describes Heaven as consisting of Major Heaven and Minor Heaven. To give my teachings more philosophical coherence, I have also removed many parts that I found had been written from the perspective of Minor Heaven, including some descriptions of the spirit world, sets of values, and historical views. Similarly, while I used the word *god* throughout the original edition, I have used the word *Buddha* in this edition to more precisely express the Buddha's teachings.

I have plans to publish more of my teachings soon, so if you would like to learn more of the basic teachings that I offer through Happy Science, I hope that you will look forward to reading my future works.

Ryuho Okawa
Founder and CEO
Happy Science Group
June 1994

ENDNOTES

Author's Note

1. In 1994, *The Laws of the Sun* went through a major revision that added several dozen pages to the first Japanese edition because much has transpired since I wrote the first edition. My reasons are twofold. First, my enlightenment has made much progress. Second, Happy Science, which has grown into one of the most influential organizations in Japan today, did not exist when I wrote the first edition, and I did not yet have a single follower. I spent dozens of hours in thorough investigation of the spirit world to create the 1994 edition, and during this process, I discovered many new and valuable facts. While the first Japanese edition explained the spirit world as a simple dichotomy between Heaven and Hell, the revised edition identifies different sides within Heaven—Major Heaven and Minor Heaven. To more accurately reflect the truth, I have removed previous interpretations of the history, perspectives, and values of the Minor Heaven. I have also replaced religious jargon with commonly used terminology so that the book might speak to a broader audience. Another revision was made in 2011.

Chapter One: The Sun of the Truths Is Rising

2. Since the emergence of Happy Science, a fifth religious movement of an unprecedented size has begun in Japan. (However, the followings of most religious groups other than Happy Science have not grown. In addition, the Happy Science movement is distinctly separate from Aum Shinrikyo and the Unification Church, who have caused social controversy.) Happy Science is a spiritual

movement devoted to countering the atheistic, materialistic values of Japanese postwar society. It is an advanced religion that provides clear guidelines for the spiritual benefit of future societies and civilizations.

Happy Science is now growing into the fourth world religion, alongside Buddhism, Christianity, and Islam. This vigorous spiritual movement will help unify these three world religions, help overcome differences, and establish Buddha's Truths on a global scale.

The first religious movement in Japan occurred between the end of the Edo period and the beginning of the Meiji period, when new religions such as Kurozumi-kyō, Konkō-kyō and Tenrikyō were active. The second movement, included new religions such as the Ōmoto-kyō, which thrived during the Taishō period and the beginning of the Shōwa period. The third movement took place after Japan's defeat in World War II, when such an abundance of new religions appeared that this period is sometimes called "the rush hour of the gods." The fourth movement occurred in the 1970s as a reaction of anxiety to Japan's rapidly growing economy and pollution problems. Psychic religions, including the GLA, Mahikari, and Agon-shū, became very popular. Although this movement gave momentum to the rise of the age of spiritualism, it also created all kinds of false beliefs, establishing the need for the religious revolution of Happy Science.

3. Shakyamuni Buddha's acknowledgement of the existence of the spirit world is clearly stated in many Buddhist scriptures. It is found in the Agama Sutras, in the stories of Shakyamuni Buddha's battle with the devil and brahma's plea to him to preach the Truths. It is also found in the "Step-by-Step Teaching," which teaches that making offerings and following the precepts gives one admittance to Heaven. Although Shakyamuni Buddha did not teach this himself, the teaching is still evident in traditional Buddhism; for example, in the teaching of the twelve links of causality in relation to our past, present, and future lives. (See *The Challenge of Enlightenment*. Sphere, 2006)

More proof can be found in the teachings of nirvana and of emptiness, in the story of Shakyamuni Buddha's birth—his descent into his mother's womb from Heaven in the form of a white elephant—and in the story of his sermon for his departed mother, Queen Maya, in the spirit world. Additionally, the Lotus Sutra contains the promise of his disciples' attainment of Buddhahood in future lives. Some erring Buddhist scholars mistakenly interpret Shakyamuni Buddha's teaching of egolessness in a materialistic way, but these are dire misinterpretations. (See, for example, *The Challenge of Enlightenment*. Sphere, 2006)

Chapter Two: Buddha's Truths Speak

4. According to Chi-i's teaching, all people originally belong to one of the Ten Worlds in the spirit world. The Ten Worlds are realms of Hell, Hunger, Animality, Anger, Humanity, Heaven, Learning, Realization, Bodhisattvahood, and Buddhahood. Everyone belongs to one of these realms, but it is also possible for us to attune our minds to any of the ten realms while we live in this world. Thus, ten types of people can have access to ten types of minds—so effectively, there are one hundred types of minds altogether. In addition to these one hundred types of mind, all things can be defined according to the following Ten Factors: 1) appearance; 2) nature; 3) entity; 4) energy; 5) influence; 6) internal cause; 7) conditions; 8) latent effect; 9) manifest effect and 10) the interrelation of factors one to nine.

When we multiply the ten realms, the ten types of mind, and the ten factors of existence, we get a total of one thousand worlds. What's more, there are three Realms of Existence: 1) Other: the world of human relationships; 2) Self: the world of the individual, which has five aspects: matter, feelings, perception, volition, and consciousness; and 3) Environment: the society, community or state. When we factor in these variations, the total number of worlds is three thousand.

This is only a brief summary of the theory behind the concept expressed as "the mind can attune to three thousand worlds." This philosophy is very Chinese in its ideology, but essentially it illustrates the ever-changing nature of the human mind. Since there are as many as three thousand kinds of minds, there is no limit to the number of thoughts that can arise. For a more detailed explanation, please refer to Chih-i's works, *Hokkegengi* ("The Essentials of the Lotus Sutra") and *Mahashikan* ("Mahayana Practice of Calming and Contemplation").

Chapter Three: The River of God's Love

5. The three negative mental functions, or worldly desires, that hurt one's divine nature are known as the Three Poisons of the Mind; they consist of greed, anger, and ignorance. Combined with conceit, doubt, and false views, they make up the Six Primary Afflictions. Traditional Buddhism teaches that the Six Primary Afflictions are the major delusions that lead people away from Right Thought and toward Hell. However, as the Buddhist expression "human

beings have 108 worldly desires" suggests, there are numerous negative mental functions. Therefore, there is no limit to how deeply we must practice Right Thought.

Chapter Four: The Ultimate Enlightenment

6. According to Japan's oldest chronicle, Kojiki ("Records of Ancient Matters"), compiled in 712 CE, Ameno-minakanushi-no-kami is the fundamental God, or the supreme God of the universe who governs the worlds of gods. However, it is hard to believe that Ō-no-Yasumaro, the author of Kojiki, and Hieda-no-Are, a psychic supporter, would have been able to understand the truths of the Creation of the universe and the fundamental God of the universe. It is more logical to interpret Kojiki as a legend that tells the stories of great figures who once lived in prehistoric Japan. In fact, I discovered through extensive research of the spirit world that Ameno-minakanushi-no-kami incarnated on Earth around 830 BCE. He built and governed an empire in Kyushu, the southern island of Japan, and is an ancestor of the present Imperial family. Currently, he resides in the upper realm of eighth dimension and is the leader of the Shinto gods. (Refer to *The Golden Laws*. Lantern Books, 2003)

Author's Note was compiled from the following lecture:

"Taiyō no Hō Nyūmon"
March 21, 2010 at Tokyo Shōshinkan in Tokyo, Japan

ABOUT THE AUTHOR

MASTER RYUHO OKAWA started receiving spiritual messages from Heaven in 1981. Holy beings appeared before him with impassioned messages of urgency, entreating him to deliver God's words to Earth. Within the same year, Master Okawa's deepest subconscious awakened and revealed his calling to become a spiritual leader who is inspiring the world with the power of God's Truths. Through these conversations with divine beings and through profound spiritual contemplation, Master Okawa developed the philosophy that would become the core of his teachings. His communications with Heaven deepened his understanding of God's designs and intentions—how He created our souls, this world, the other world, and the Laws that are the very fabric of the universe. In 1986, Master Okawa founded Happy Science to share God's Truths and to help humankind overcome religious and cultural conflicts and usher in an era of peace on Earth. The universality and integrity of his spiritual teachings, delivered in his uniquely simple and pragmatic way, have

have attracted millions of readers and followers in over one hundred countries. In addition to publishing over one thousand three hundred books, Master Okawa has delivered more than two thousand talks and lectures, and continues to share God's Truths throughout the world.

ABOUT HAPPY SCIENCE

In 1986, Master Ryuho Okawa founded Happy Science, a spiritual movement dedicated to bringing greater happiness to humankind by overcoming barriers of race, religion, and culture and by working toward the ideal of a world united in peace and harmony. Supported by followers who live in accordance with Master Okawa's words of enlightened wisdom, Happy Science has grown rapidly since its beginnings in Japan and now extends throughout the world. Today, it has twelve million members around the globe, with faith centers in New York, Los Angeles, San Francisco, Tokyo, London, Sydney, Sao Paulo, and Hong Kong, among many other major cities. Master Okawa speaks at Happy Science centers and travels around the world giving public lectures. Happy Science provides a variety of programs and services to support local communities. These programs include preschools, after-school educational programs for youths, and services for senior citizens and the disabled. Members also participate in social and charitable activities, which in the past have included providing relief aid to earthquake victims in China, New Zealand, and Turkey, and to flood victims in Thailand as well as building schools in Sri Lanka.

Programs and Events

Happy Science faith centers offer regular events, programs, and seminars. Join our meditation sessions, video lectures, study groups, seminars, and book events. Our programs will help you:

- Deepen your understanding of the purpose and meaning of life
- Improve your relationships as you learn how to love unconditionally
- Learn how to calm your mind even on stressful days through the practice of contemplation and meditation
- Learn how to overcome life's challenges
  . . . and much more.

International Seminars

Each year, friends from all over the world join our international seminars, held at our faith centers in Japan. Different programs are offered each year and cover a wide variety of topics, including improving relationships, practicing the Eightfold Path to enlightenment, and loving yourself, to name just a few.

Happy Science Monthly

Read Master Okawa's latest lectures in our monthly booklet, Happy Science Monthly. You'll also find stories of members' life-changing experiences, news from Happy Science members around the world, in-depth information about Happy Science movies, book reviews, and much more. Happy Science Monthly is available in English, Portuguese, Chinese, and other languages. Back issues are available upon request. Subscribe by contacting the Happy Science location nearest you.

CONTACT INFORMATION

Happy Science is a worldwide organization with faith centers around the globe. For a comprehensive list of centers, visit the worldwide directory at www.happy-science.org or www.happyscience-usa.org.

The following are some of the many Happy Science locations:

United States and Canada

NEW YORK
79 Franklin Street,
New York, NY 10013
Phone: 212-343-7972
Fax: 212-343-7973
Email: ny@happy-science.org
Website: www.happyscience-ny.org

LOS ANGELES
1590 E. Del Mar Blvd.,
Pasadena, CA 91106
Phone: 626-395-7775
Fax: 626-395-7776
Email: la@happy-science.org
Website: www.happyscience-la.org

SAN DIEGO
Email: sandiego@happy-science.org

SAN FRANCISCO
525 Clinton Street,
Redwood City, CA 94062
Phone/Fax: 650-363-2777
Email: sf@happy-science.org
Website: www.happyscience-sf.org

FLORIDA
12208 N 56th Street,
Temple Terrace, FL 33617
Phone:813-914-7771
Fax: 813-914-7710
Email: florida@happy-science.org
Website: www.happyscience-fl.org

NEW JERSEY
725 River Road, Suite 200,
Edgewater, NJ 07025
Phone: 201-313-0127
Fax: 201-313-0120
Email: nj@happy-science.org
Website: www.happyscience-nj.org

ATLANTA
1893 Piedmont Road,
Atlanta, GA 30324
Phone/Fax: 404-963-6781
Email: atlanta@happy-science.org
Website: www.happyscience-atlanta.org

HAWAII
1221 Kapiolani Blvd., Suite 920,
Honolulu, HI 96814
Phone: 808-591-9772
Fax: 808-591-9776
Email: hi@happy-science.org
Website: www.happyscience-hi.org

KAUAI
4504 Kukui Street,
Dragon Building Suite 21,
P. O. Box 1060
Kapaa, HI 96746
Phone: 808-822-7007
Fax: 808-822-6007
Email: kauai-hi@happy-science.org
Website: www.happyscience-kauai.org

TORONTO
323 College Street,
Toronto ON M5T 1S2, Canada
Phone/Fax: 1-416-901-3747
Email: toronto@happy-science.org
Website: www.happy-science.ca

VANCOUVER
#212-2609 East 49th Avenue,
Vancouver, V5S 1J9, Canada
Phone: 1-604-437-7735
Fax: 1-604-437-7764
Email: vancouver@happy-science.org
Website: www.happy-science.ca

International

TOKYO
1-6-7 Togoshi, Shinagawa,
Tokyo, 142-0041 Japan
Phone: 81-3-6384-5770
Fax: 81-3-6384-5776
Email: tokyo@happy-science.org
Website: www.happy-science.org

LONDON
3 Margaret Street,
London, W1W 8RE, United Kingdom
Phone: 44-20-7323-9255
Fax: 44-20-7323-9344
Email: eu@happy-science.org
Website: www.happyscience-uk.org

SYDNEY
516 Pacific Hwy, Lane Cove North,
2066 NSW Australia
Phone: 61-2-9411-2877
Fax: 61-2-9411-2822
Email: aus@happy-science.org
Website: www.happyscience.org.au

BRAZIL HEADQUARTERS
Rua. Domingos de Morais 1154,
Vila Mariana, Sao Paulo, CEP 04009-002, Brazil
Phone: 55-11-5088-3800
Fax: 55-11-5088-3806
Email: sp@happy-science.org
Website: www.happyscience-br.org

SEOUL
162-17 Sadang3-dong,
Dongjak-gu, Seoul, Korea
Phone: 82-2-3478-8777
Fax: 82-2-3478-9777
Email: korea@happy-science.org
Website: www.happyscience-korea.org

TAIPEI
No. 89, Lane 155, Dunhua N. Road,
Songshan District, Taipei City 105, Taiwan
Phone: 886-2-2719-9377
Fax: 886-2-2719-5570
Email: taiwan@happy-science.org
Website: www.happyscience-tw.org

UGANDA

Plot 877 Rubaga Road, Kampala,

P.O. Box 34130, Kampala, Uganda

Phone: 256-78-4728-601

Email: uganda@happy-science.org

Website: www.happyscience-uganda.org

ABOUT IRH PRESS

IRH Press Co., Ltd, based in Tokyo, was founded in 1987 as a publishing division of Happy Science. IRH Press publishes religious and spiritual books, journals, and magazines, and also operates broadcast and film-production enterprises. For more information, visit www.OkawaBooks.com.

OTHER BOOKS
BY RYUHO OKAWA

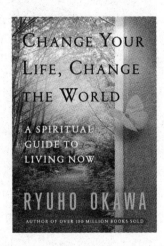

CHANGE YOUR LIFE, CHANGE THE WORLD
A Spiritual Guide to Living Now
ISBN: 978-0-9826985-0-I
$16.95 (Paperback)

MASTER RYUHO OKAWA calls out to people of all nations to remember their true spiritual roots and to build our planet into a united Earth of peace, prosperity, and happiness. With the spiritual wisdom contained in this book, each and every one of us can change our lives and change the world.

"To save the seven billion people on Earth, God has countless angels working constantly, every day, on His behalf." —Chapter 3

THE MOMENT OF TRUTH
Become a Living Angel Today
ISBN: 978-0-9826985-7-0
$14.95 (Paperback)

MASTER OKAWA shows that we are essentially spiritual beings and that our true and lasting happiness is not found within the material world but rather in acts of unconditional and selfless love toward the greater world. These pages reveal God's mind, His mercy, and His hope that many of us will become living angels that shine light onto this world.

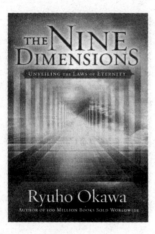

THE NINE DIMENSIONS

Unveiling the Laws of Eternity

ISBN: 978-0-9826985-6-3

$15.95 (Paperback)

THIS BOOK IS YOUR GATE TO HEAVEN. In this book, Master Okawa shows that God designed this world and the vast, wondrous world of our afterlife as a school with many levels through which our souls learn and grow. This book is a window into the mind of our loving God, who encourages us to grow into greater angels.

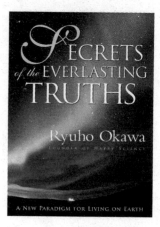

SECRETS OF THE EVERLASTING TRUTHS
A New Paradigm for Living on Earth
ISBN: 978-1-937673-10-9
$14.95 (Paperback)

OUR BELIEF IN THE INVISIBLE IS OUR FUTURE.
It is our knowledge about the everlasting spiritual laws and
our belief in the invisible that will make it possible for us to
solve the world's problems and bring our entire planet together. When you discover the secrets in this book, your view
of yourself and the world will be changed dramatically and
forever.

ALSO BY RYUHO OKAWA

THE SCIENCE OF HAPPINESS
10 Principles for Manifesting Your Divine Nature

THE GOLDEN LAWS
History through the Eyes of the Eternal Buddha

THE STARTING POINT OF HAPPINESS
A Practical and Intuitive Guide to Discovering Love, Wisdom, and Faith

LOVE, NURTURE, AND FORGIVE
A Handbook to Add a New Richness to Your Life

AN UNSHAKABLE MIND
How to Overcome Life's Difficulties

THE ORIGIN OF LOVE
On the Beauty of Compassion

INVINCIBLE THINKING
There Is No Such Thing as Defeat

GUIDEPOSTS TO HAPPINESS
Prescriptions for a Wonderful Life

THE LAWS OF HAPPINESS
The Four Principles for a Successful Life

TIPS TO FIND HAPPINESS
Creating a Harmonious Home for Your Spouse,
Your Children, and Yourself

THE PHILOSOPHY OF PROGRESS
Higher Thinking for Developing Infinite Prosperity

THE ESSENCE OF BUDDHA
The Path to Enlightenment

THE CHALLENGE OF THE MIND
A Practical Approach to the Essential Buddhist Teaching of Karma

THE CHALLENGE OF ENLIGHTENMENT
Realize Your Inner Potential